Kickstarter for the Independent Creator

A Practical and Informative Guide to Crowdfunding

Written by an Independent Creator for Independent Creators

By M. Holly-Rosing

Copyright © 2015 and 2017 Madeleine Holly-Rosing
Cover design by Christie Shinn of HoraTora Studios

Edited by Barbra Dillon

Published By Brass-T Publishing

2nd Edition 2017

All Rights Reserved

ISBN 978-0-9964292-3-8 (pbk)
ISBN 978-0-9964292-4-5 (ebk)

DEDICATION

This book is dedicated to my Kickstarter backers. Without you, Boston Metaphysical Society Comic would not have been possible.

***

Special thanks to Mark Stokes, Sarah Roark, George Wassil, and my husband David Rosing.

CONTENTS

DISCLAIMER

No part of this publication may be reproduced, stored in a retrieval system, or transmitted in any form or by any means, electronic, mechanical, photocopying, recording, scanning, or otherwise, except as permitted under Sections 107 or 108 of the 1976 United States Copyright Act, without prior written permission of the publisher.

Trademarks: Kickstarter is a trademark of Kickstarter, Inc. All other trademarks are the property of their respective owners. Brass-T Publishing is not associated with any product or vendor mentioned in this book.

Limit of Liability/Disclaimer of Warranty: The publisher and the author make no representations or warranties with respect to the accuracy or completeness of the contents of this work and specifically disclaim all warranties, including without limitation warranties of fitness for a particular purpose. No warranty may be created or extended by sales or promotional materials. The advice and strategies contained herein may not be suitable for every situation. This work is sold with the understanding that the publisher is not engaged in rendering legal, accounting, or other professional services. If professional assistance is required, the services of a competent professional person should be sought. Neither the publisher nor the author shall be liable for damages arising herefrom. The fact that an organization or website is referred to in this work as a citation and/or a potential source of further information does not mean that the author or publisher endorses the information the organization or website may provide nor recommendations it may make. Further, readers should be aware that internet websites listed in this work may change or disappear between when this work was written and when it is read.

FOREWORD

If you're reading this book, the future success of your crowdfunding project is in good hands.

I remember doing extensive research on comic books that were being crowdfunded before I gave it a go, yet I was still completely unprepared. Before I launched my first Kickstarter, I read some blogs and notes from people who either successfully funded their own or failed trying, hoping to prepare for the madness that lay ahead. I still wasn't.

In 2013 I was asked by Clydene Nee (a wonderful woman I met online that helped me get a panel at San Diego Comic-Con that year) to do a spotlight on people that ran Kickstarters. I used the opportunity to learn more, having a filmmaker, a musician, a video game designer, and a comic book creator join me, knowing they could impart a bit of wisdom (or at least their own experiences, good and bad) to the crowd, and to me.

After walking off that panel, I remember hoping that someone out there that had gone through those same experiences crowdfunding would teach classes on it, and maybe compile those experiences into a great guide for people who were as lost as I was in the beginning. Now granted, more than a few people have written about and taught classes on crowdfunding, but none that match the passion and creativity of Madeleine Holly-Rosing.

Most people that have an unsuccessful crowdfunding project will give up, walk away, and never try again. The reason is a valid one. As someone who pitches stories on a daily basis, only to face rejection, I at least am only getting the rejection from one editor or one publisher. When a Kickstarter fails, there's a chance you will feel like the whole world has rejected you.

In the following pages, Madeleine explains how that's not the case. She's your coach, teacher, and guide. She tells you some things that you may not want to admit you did wrong, but she does it so that it's easier for you to pick yourself back up and try again, knowing what to do differently this time around. Like a great coach, she breaks down the obstacles you will face from every angle. Like a great teacher, she provides lessons that will expand your creative mind into something that mine naturally wants to resist, but knows it needs desperately, which is how to market your product. And as a great guide, she will lead you to success.

The world needs more creativity from those of us who don't have the resources, fame, and money to make it happen on our own. We do, however, have the one thing we need the most: passion. Read this book carefully and learn from it. The future success of your project is in the very best of hands: Madeleine's... and your own.

Good luck!

-Siike Donnelly (5/26/15)
Siike is a writer, editor, and artist living in Los Angeles with his rescue dog, Echo. He urges you to send your project to him when it's active via Twitter (@ExplodingBullet), so he can help you spread the word.

INTRODUCTION

Like most writers/creators, I have a story to tell. And this one will sound very familiar to every independent creator out there. To get our comics, films, web series, or any creative endeavor we are passionate about done and out there in the world costs money. Fortunately for us, Kickstarter and other crowdfunding platforms were developed to help us do just that. But what they don't tell you is that in order to be successful at it, you can't just throw something up on Kickstarter or Indiegogo and hope backers will come. No. Sorry. Not going to happen unless you are celebrity, and even then I've seen some of those projects crash and burn.

I know. I've been there.

My project was a six-issue mini-series called *Boston Metaphysical Society* (A Steampunk Comic). It started as a webcomic which my husband and I self-financed for the first three issues. I was doing well at conventions, and we had a pretty decent online readership, so we felt we could launch a Kickstarter to fund the art production and printing of the last three issues and compile all six issues into a nice paperback trade. The goal was $25,000, which is not unreasonable if you know the comics business. (If you don't, this amount would barely cover paying my artist, colorist, letterer, production, printing, shipping, Amazon/Kickstarter fees, and rewards.)

What I didn't realize was that most of the people who read the comic online would not contribute, and that I hadn't really built up a big enough following through conventions. What I also learned is that Kickstarter had also lost some of its shiny newness, and backers were tired of getting burned by projects that were never completed. And even though I had an okay social media presence at the time, I had not really put together a serious email list of potential backers to help get the word out. So, assumptions piled onto mistakes led to disaster—but did it?

Though that particular Kickstarter campaign failed to reach its goal, I learned a lot by watching how other people handled failing and doing (or not doing) some of the things they did. I learned that backers were more willing to pledge to a comic or a project that was finished, or at least almost completed. The comic got a lot more publicity, which helped. I was also able to put together that all-important core backer email list, which we'll discuss more in a later section, and I did a much better job doing what I refer to as "Pre-Launch Strategy" and developing a strategy for the course of the campaign the second time around.

I re-launched three months later. The project was fully funded in less than 48 hours.

The goal was only $3,000.00 this time, but we ended up at $7,060.00 and met four stretch goals. Our third Kickstarter goal of $7,500.00 was to fund the art production and printing of Chapter 5. We reached $8,260.00. The fourth had a goal of $3,200.00 and by the time the campaign ended, we had reached $6,647.00 and I did it without the use of a paid social media expert or a PR person. It was just me, sitting in front of my computer with my husband who made sure I was fed, watered, and got to sleep.

Afterwards, it got me thinking… I've seen so many terrific projects not make their funding goal. With more preparation and an understanding of how this all works, I decided to share what I had learned, and I reached out to one of my local comic book stores to see if we could partner up to teach a class. Mike Lerner at Pulp Fiction Books and Comics in Culver City was game when I told him my background, which includes marketing and teaching. He was all in, so we launched the first ever Crowdfunding Class for Independent Creators.

The idea behind the class was to teach independent creators how to organize and prepare a practical strategy for running a Kickstarter campaign for under or around $10,000 without having to rely on or pay someone else. Having been in the trenches myself, I knew it could be done. The reasons I focused on a goal of $10,000 or less were, firstly, that was my experience, and secondly, when you start raising the funding goal to $15,000 and above, you really need a dedicated team of people on board to make that happen. It's a very different organizational dynamic. This book is an expanded version of that class in an easy-to-carry format.

Since crowdfunding is such a large part of the comics and creator community, I'm going to assume you have a basic knowledge of Kickstarter and Indiegogo – meaning, you have either backed a Kickstarter or know people who have.

Even though my personal experience is in crowdfunding a comic, all of the information and strategies I discuss are applicable to any type of independent creator project: jewelry, widgets, fashion accessories, book editing, short films, music CDs, etc.

So, hold on tight and let's dive into what will be your second full-time job.

INTRODUCTION TO THE SECOND EDITION

I've been wanting to write this second edition for awhile, but I decided to wait until I finished my 2017 campaign. I'm so glad I did, as I learned even more in this rapidly changing industry known as crowdfunding. It's been an exciting time, and I'm happy that this book has helped so many people be successful at funding their projects. But I'm not one to sit back and let things ride. I'm always looking to make everything I do better and more useful to you.

Having worked with independent creators in a wide variety of industries (film, comics, music, and literature) over the past two years, I wanted to make this book more accessible to them. Therefore, I've expanded and altered the focus of the first chapter to discuss how to choose your crowdfunding platform, added chapters on taxes and handling success, as well as added and updated almost every chapter along with references to other campaigns and podcast/interview sites. It was a challenge to keep this book focused on the essentials, as crowdfunding has developed into big business.

Every strategy in this book applies to any type of crowdfunding project, large or small; however, if you are looking for a funding goal of over $20,000, then there is an organizational dynamic involved which this book does not cover. This book is designed specifically for the entrepreneurial independent creator who dreams big, but knows you have to start small to get there.

Wishing you all the best,

Madeleine Holly-Rosing (April 2017)

CHAPTER 1.

CHOOSING A PLATFORM

Selecting a crowdfunding platform that's best for you depends on your project and campaign goals. There are many crowdfunding platforms out there, but let's start with the three which I feel are doing the best job for the independent creator at this point in time. Crowdfunding is constantly evolving, so there is a good chance this list may change in the future.

Before we get into discussing the platforms, here are a few questions to consider when choosing the right one for you:

- Does your project appeal to a crowdfunding audience?
- Does the platform complement your project?
- Does the platform support your particular type of project?

KICKSTARTER

I've run five campaigns on Kickstarter and found it to be easy to use and the perfect platform for comics. Some of the important elements of Kickstarter include:

1. Since it's been around the longest, it has more caché than any other platform.
2. Kickstarter has the largest community of followers.
3. Backers feel more confident pledging their money to

Kickstarter, knowing they will not be charged unless the project meets its goal.

4. You will get more publicity through Kickstarter than any other crowdfunding platform.
5. Kickstarter has a well-established reputation.
6. You can now launch campaigns from Canada, the U.K., Australia, New Zealand, the Netherlands, Denmark, Ireland, Norway, Sweden, and Germany. No doubt more countries will be added over time.
7. It only allows creative projects.
8. The "All or Nothing" concept is very exciting to backers and can lead to larger pledges.
9. Most successful projects have a funding goal of under $10,000.
10. The Community Tab allows not only you to see who your backers are and where they hail from, but how many are new or returning backers.
11. New Kickstarter Live program allows you to live stream to your backers.

I did not use Kickstarter Live in my last campaign, but I know a few people who did and did not find it to be terribly effective. The idea behind it is that you can stream directly to your backers who can ask questions and interact with you. As a creator, you can show them your process and talk about your crowdfunding strategies, rewards, etc. It's up to you how you want to use it. Since it is so new, I think it's just finding its footing and will eventually find its way into the process.

INDIEGOGO

Indiegogo has many things going for it, as well:

1. It has several funding choices which include flexible funding. Flexible funding means you don't need to meet your goal in order to get your money. (Be sure to read the

details on the different fees they charge for each type of funding.)

2. It is a very reputable crowdfunding platform.
3. It seems to be favored by films and other unique projects, especially non-profits, and accepts all types of projects.
4. You have the option to extend your campaign.
5. They now have equity crowdfunding options.
6. Backers can pledge to multiple tiers. (I love this option, and I wish Kickstarter allowed it.)
7. InDemand Program – A completed, successful campaign on Indiegogo or Kickstarter can continue their campaign for an indefinite amount of time. It is essentially a pre-order system. (Be aware that higher fees apply to this program.)

After my last campaign, I was approached by Indiegogo to become part of their InDemand Program. I decided it would be a great opportunity to test it out, so I agreed and launched in March 2017. I haven't gotten much traction on it, but, to be fair, I have spent very little time promoting it. (And I mean very little time.) I know other creators who have done well, but I don't have the time and energy to spend on it. We'll see how it goes; however, I wasn't too keen on the organization of the backend, as it required me to save information twice and how they defined "perks" vs. "items" seemed redundant. I felt it caused me more work than necessary.

The Indiegogo community is much smaller than Kickstarter's and is less dedicated. Also, if you choose flexible funding and don't make your goal, backers still may expect to receive their rewards. Then, you are stuck with either ponying up the money to send out rewards you didn't expect to buy, or trying to fend off annoyed or potentially angry backers.

SEED&SPARK (For Film Only)

Seed&Spark launched in 2012 and had a few hiccups along the

way, but has evolved into what I think is a terrific platform for filmmakers. The organization of their website with the tabs right below the video is simple and elegant. I have not personally used this platform, but I've been studying it for awhile and what I see impresses me.

Here are the highlights:

1. Campaigns are considered funded at 80%.
2. Like Kickstarter, backers are not charged if you do not make 80% of your funding goal.
3. Wishlist and reward tier incentives.
4. Distribution network for creators with 500+ followers.
5. Fiscal and partner Opportunities.
6. Potential marketing opportunities through their platform.
7. Pays out in a week.
8. Exceptional creator's guide and videos.
9. They are building a strong community of backers.

If you aren't familiar with their platform, a "Wishlist" is in addition to the traditional reward tiers. As a creator, you can list specific items or help you need that backers can either donate to or contribute/loan their time and equipment. Some examples would be: a colorist, a composer, a location, props, etc. I think it's a great idea.

They also have exceptionally good "How to Crowdfund" videos that are applicable to any crowdfunding campaign.

OTHER PLATFORMS

What about Patreon, you ask?

I think Patreon is a terrific platform, but its model is not for everyone. If you are not familiar with the site, the idea behind it is that your "Patron" pays a certain amount per month and receives something for that level of backing. It's a great idea for artists, vloggers, and web series, or something where you control the delivery date, but doesn't work quite so well for writers unless you are extremely prolific, have an editor on staff, or are already famous. Good time management skills are required, as you must deliver rewards regularly.

The other challenge, which may change in time, is that you must bring your backers with you. Unlike Kickstarter, Patreon does not have a community of followers who search out campaigns to back. That means you have to spend time promoting your Patreon campaign, which does not have the urgency behind it like a campaign on Kickstarter or Indiegogo does.

There is also GoFundMe, but it is primarily used for personal and charity events. There are a host of other crowdfunding platforms for nonprofits, real estate, and equity crowdfunding, but that's a topic for another book.

Remember, the rules, policies, and fees of all these crowdfunding platforms do change over time, so be sure you read the fine print and make sure you understand it before launching.

CHAPTER 2.

BEFORE YOU LAUNCH

WEBSITES

This may be obvious, but you need a website for your project. You would be surprised at the number of people I have consulted with that were itching to launch and did not have a website up yet. Let me be very clear—you must have a website for your project.

I am not a website expert, but here are a few things I'd recommend:

1. Research websites that are similar to your project and figure out what you like and don't like. For instance, many webcomics are heavy into advertising, and it can make the site looked cluttered. Resist the urge to do that, as you won't make that much money from it anyway. If you find a website you like, contact the creator and ask who designed it. Referrals might get you a discount.

2. Be sure to buy your domain name and variations of that name and have them redirected to your main website.

3. If you can't afford either of the above, you can use sites like Tapastic to host your comic for free until you've got enough money to pay for your own site.

4. Shop around. There are many companies that sell domain names and host websites. (Register.com and GoDaddy, to name a few.)

BUILDING A SOCIAL MEDIA PRESENCE

It's time to set up your social media accounts, if you haven't already.

TWITTER

Sign up for an account at www.twitter.com. You might want to consider setting up a personal account and a project account. (I wish I had done that myself when I first launched *Boston Metaphysical Society* as a webcomic. As a writer, I know that in the future it will not be my only project.) Make sure you upload a profile picture and cover that represents your project. Start following fellow creators, publishers, podcasts, reviewers, and basically anyone you think is interesting and that you honestly think would be interested in your project. Twitter allows you to create lists, so you can organize fellow creators, podcasters, etc. into lists. I would suggest naming the lists fun and cool names i.e., (Most Freakin' Awesome Podcaster, etc.). The reason I suggest you add people to a list, is that they are notified when they are added to the list and they may come and check your profile out and follow you back if the name piques their interest. Lists can be public or private. You can also create additional accounts, so you can retweet your project without it looking like you are retweeting yourself.

As with all social media, tweet fun things, interesting articles, and join in conversations without being a stalker. Adding a picture increases your chances of being retweeted. Retweet others generously, and over time start making friends and be sure to thank people for retweeting you. It also doesn't hurt if you add your newfound friends' handles to #FF (Follow Friday) on Fridays. If you are not familiar with hashtags, they are used to mark keywords or topics. According to Twitter, it was "created organically by Twitter users as a way to categorize messages."

Don't go too crazy with the hashtags, but be sure to use them as they help when people search by topic. As with all social media, be polite, courteous, and use this opportunity to make friends. Hopefully, these will be some of the people who will either back or help promote your project.

FACEBOOK

If you don't already have a Facebook page, you can sign up for one at www.facebook.com. I have two Facebook pages: one that's personal and one for the comic. I would suggest you do that, as well. My comic Facebook page is technically a book series page. (It used to be an "Author" page, but it made sense to change it.) The reason I selected the book series designation is that it allows me to add tabs for a store, videos, Twitter, author app, and more. Whatever designation you select is up to you, but you need a page dedicated to your project.

You should also join like-minded Facebook groups, as well. In my case, there are a wide variety of comic and steampunk groups based throughout the world. If your project is a short film, you could join film groups. The same thing if you're making jewelry or any type of creative project. Once you join these groups, be sure to read the rules and follow them to the letter. If you have a question, ask the moderator. Some groups allow shameless self-promotion while others require you to limit it to once a month. There are also groups that are strictly informational in nature. It's important to be reasonably active in these groups in order to build your street cred and make friends with other creators who probably know more than you do. Post articles that might be of real interest to the group and don't ask questions like, "How can I get more 'likes' or 'followers.'" That's just annoying.

We'll go into how you can use Facebook as part of your campaign in a later section.

LINKEDIN

I've heard mixed reviews on the usefulness of LinkedIn, but I know it has been somewhat useful to me to establish myself as not only a comic creator, but a reviewer and interviewer as well. As you've probably guessed, you can sign up at www.linkedin.com. I would also suggest joining the various groups related to your background and project and set up your profile so it looks professional.

I don't spend a lot of time on LinkedIn, but if I have a new review, interview, or something pertinent to announce, I will post it. I've only gotten a handful of Kickstarter backers through Linkedin, but I have sold books and made some good business contacts.

GOOGLE+

Get a Google+ account. Not because anyone actually reads Google+ posts, but you need the account in order to have a YouTube account. A YouTube account is critical in order to post your video and use it as a platform. Be sure to get a custom URL for your project. Go to YouTube settings, click on "Advanced," and then click on "Create Custom URL."

You do want to post articles, updates, and fun things on Google+ periodically just to make sure you get into the search engines, and, besides, you never know who might be watching.

TUMBLR

Tumblr has its own unique vibe and is driven by pictures, memes, cartoons, and pretty much anything visual. You will occasionally get long blogs that expound on the nature of, well, whatever, but it is primarily a visual medium and does not lend itself to promotion of any kind. Others may have had a different experience. You can sign up for an account at www.tumblr.com.

REDDIT

I have mixed feelings about Reddit (www.reddit.com). Not being a heavy user, I can't really say it's done much to promote my comic or the Kickstarter. I suspect it's because my comic is really a graphic novel and it's not a great venue for that kind of project. On the other hand, I know that the strip comic *Lunarbaboon* has a huge Reddit following, as do other strip-format comics. I heard through my various social media contacts that the creator of *Lunarbaboon* spent a lot of time building a Reddit following and I know it paid off when he ran his Kickstarter. Like with most things, you get what you put into it.

INSTAGRAM

I used Instagram a bit more in my last campaign, but it was not part of my overall marketing strategy when I launched; however, I'm not sure how much good it did. They recently launched Instagram Video Live which a friend of mine, Russell Nohelty from Wannabee Press, experimented with in his last few campaigns and had more viewers than on Facebook Live and Kickstarter Live combined. (www.instagram.com)

I primarily use Facebook and Twitter to promote and cross-promote, as I don't have time to focus on every social media account (and you won't either). And yes, I know there are apps out there that help you manage and link several accounts at once, but I like to choose the specific times and groups I post to while running a campaign so it doesn't look spammy.

BUILDING YOUR ONLINE PRESENCE

Once your social media accounts are set up (whichever ones you decide to focus on), it's time to get serious about how you are going to use them. I can't stress enough about how important it is to follow or friend other fellow creators and those who may be interested in the type of work you do. Make friends and be nice. Though they may not back your Kickstarter, they will probably retweet, repost, or reblog about it.

GUEST BLOGS

One of the best ways to promote your work without it seeming like you are promoting yourself is by writing guest blogs and/or reviews, or interviews. I have written guest blogs for Steampunk Coffee Time Romance, Steamed!, Emma Jane Holloway's author website, and a number of others. In addition, I do reviews of comics and novels as well as interviews, for Fanbase Press.

Many of the guest blogs came about because I either saw their site on social media or found them through a Google search. I researched their site and once I saw they were open to guest blogs (and most people are), I contacted them to ask if I could do one. Often, they will want you to stick to a particular theme, but others will let you do pretty much what you want, as long as it's something their audience will enjoy. If you have a particular expertise that fits into their website, let them know and they will probably be thrilled to have you write a blog. The blogs are usually about 300-500 words long, and it's always good to include pictures of your work (if appropriate). Never use photos or artwork that is copyrighted by someone else without their permission.

REVIEWS AND INTERVIEWS

I was introduced to Barbra Dillon at Fanbase Press through a fellow creator while I was handing out postcards for my comic at Comikazi Expo in Los Angeles. They send out an email newsletter, like many other small press comic publishing sites, and they were very nice about promoting special events for my comic. She offered to have someone review my comic; I happily said yes. After about a year, I decided to write a review of an acquaintance's comic, and I contacted Barbra to ask if they would be interested in publishing it. She read it and said yes, and then offered to put me on as a guest contributor. (No pay is involved here.) Another year passed and they promoted me to regular contributor with my own blog. Because of this, I have met and made friends with numerous other creators, as well as added to my fan base. Plus, I get to read some terrific comics.

The point is, you can do this too with other types of small press publishers, review sites, or podcasts.

Reviews of your own work, whether it be a comic, novel, or the latest piece of jewelry, are one of the best ways to get noticed. Plus, it's a fun thing to be able to post a review on Facebook, Twitter, or other social media. (Obviously, good or at least solid reviews are preferred.) The question is, how do you find reviewers?

This is where research and making friends comes in. I started by doing Google searches on anyone who did webcomic reviews. When I exhausted that, I searched on Twitter and Facebook for comic reviewers and steampunk sites. I would visit their website, and once I decided that they were the appropriate venue, I contacted them. (Samples of contact emails are in the Appendix.) When I talk about an appropriate venue, what I mean is: do they review the type of material you create and/or write? Do they require a certain page count or issues to be completed before they look at it? For projects other than comics, they may ask how long you have been in business, or may only look at leatherwork or women's jewelry. When in doubt, ask.

The point here is that I took the time to reach out, make friends, and establish my credibility within the comic and steampunk communities. Also, many of these same websites post Kickstarter Spotlight sections. That, in itself, is worth its weight in gold.

Podcasts. These are great opportunities to reach a wider audience than you would normally have a chance to do. Podcasts are usually recorded, but are sometimes live. In the comics and/or geek world, podcasts are very popular and can be extremely useful. I have a list of comic podcasts in the Appendix, but it will be worth your while to search out more through Google, Twitter, and Facebook. Contact them like you would for any interview and see what they say. Most are busy, but are always looking for new people to spotlight.

Interviews. As with podcasts, interviews are very helpful in building a following. After you make contact with the interviewer, they usually send an email interview for you to complete by a certain date. A few will want to interview you by Skype, but I would encourage you to do the email interview if possible. That way, you can do a draft, let it sit for a few days, and then go back and tweak it. I've found that even with the best of intentions (and attention spans), it's difficult for an interviewer to remember everything you have said and you'll end up having to revise it anyway when they send it to you for review.

KICKSTARTER COMMUNITY

Kickstarter is a community, so it's critical that you become part of it. That means you must back and promote other Kickstarters before you launch your own. Be aware that once you launch, Kickstarter posts how many campaigns you have created, as well as how many you have backed. If you have backed zero, it makes you look greedy and self-serving. Don't be that person.

That doesn't mean you have to promote or back everyone, especially if it's an R-rated project and you want your posts to remain PG-13. Nor does it mean you need to spend a lot of money. A dollar pledge is greatly appreciated by most creators, and the only ones who will know how much you have pledged are the campaign creators. Use common sense and discretion. Don't make fun of other projects or denigrate them. That will make you look petty and not a team player. You are responsible for your own self-image and marketing, so be sure you establish the image you want and maintain it.

OTHER WAYS TO MINE FOR POTENTIAL BACKERS

Social media is a great way to find potential backers and costs nothing but your time; however, it is important to get out into the world so people can meet you and know that you are a real person. I know it sounds silly, but a physical handshake does more to cement a relationship than a thousand retweets, texts, and posts. And that person could be the backer that helps you achieve your funding goal.

Let me tell you a story… I met George Wassil who is the writer/creator of the graphic novel, *Oh, Hell*, in a sequential art class, where we both developed our stories and eventually hired artists, colorists, and the same letterer to produce our comics. We became friends, and in the beginning of our comic careers shared a table at conventions and traveled together quite a bit. I launched my first two Kickstarters before he ran his first campaign, so he was able to learn from some of my mistakes.

George is not a big social media person. In fact, his online presence barely registers; however, he has attended close to thirty conventions in a year and is proud to say that he has shaken hands with everyone who has liked his Facebook page. From those conventions he was able to put together an impressive email list. He launched a campaign to raise $12,500, and I was worried for him. I felt he didn't have the online presence he needed to be successful. I'm happy to say that I was wrong.

Because of the outreach he did through the conventions and the fact that 60% of his pledges came through Kickstarter sources, George was not only able to reach his goal, but he ended up raising $14,053.

Now, most of us do not possess the resources to attend that many conventions in one year, so we need to strike a balance between conventions, local events, and social media; however, you do need to make the most out of your convention time.

Here are some basic requirements to help build your fan base, who will then, hopefully, turn into backers:

Conventions (If You Have a Table)

- Know your pitch. For comic creators and novelists, this is essential. You must be able to tell your story in thirty seconds or less. (This is often called an elevator pitch.) If you are a "maker" (i.e., you make jewelry or other crafts), you'll need samples of your work. It also doesn't hurt if you have a story to tell about how you created and/or what inspired your work. Take a page from Trader Joe's marketing. Every item they sell has a story attached to it. (If you are not familiar with Trader Joe's, check out their website and you will see what I mean.)

- Have an email sign-up sheet at your table.

- Have free marketing material to give out, (i.e., postcards, bookmarks, etc.).

- Have a banner either behind you and/or on your table identifying who or what your project is.

- Be proactive at your table. Don't sit behind your table and hide or check your email. Stand up and talk to people. You can't be shy. Besides, you'll make some new friends.

- Panelist. Get on a panel or propose one. This is great exposure and will drive traffic to your table.

- Cosplayers. If you're lucky, you might eventually have people who will want to dress as the characters from your comic. If that happens, take lots of pictures and post it everywhere! (If this happens to you, consider yourself blessed.)

Conventions (Not Exhibiting)

Not ready for a table yet? Couldn't afford it or missed a deadline? No problem. Here are some things you can do to promote your project without exhibiting.

- Panels. Though you don't have a table to drive traffic to, be sure to bring postcards (or other marketing material) and let people know they can pick one up after the panel.

- Attending a panel. There will always be a panel that is somewhat related to your project. Go to it. Before the panel begins, you can place your postcards on the chairs. Sit by the back door and five minutes before the panel is over, stand outside the door and hand out postcards as people leave the room. Be polite, respectful, and don't get upset if they refuse your card. If they don't take it, remember you are not wasting money on someone not interested in your project.

- Some events will have a central location where you can leave your postcards among a bunch of others. You might even be able to find a friendly face who is willing to allow your cards on their table if you ask nicely.

By the way, conventions are not just for comic creators. If you are looking to crowdfund a movie, especially a sci-fi or fantasy one, conventions are a great way to start building a fan base. The first time I tabled at WonderCon, I shared it with a couple of colleagues who were promoting their sci-fi horror film, *5th Passenger*. They dressed in costume, had a trailer, and handed out postcards about it. Flash forward two years later, they ran a successful Kickstarter campaign to fund principal photography. The point is they started small and slowly developed a fan base. And more importantly, they did not launch until they were ready.

OTHER EVENTS (COMICS AND OTHER PROJECTS)

Signings. These are usually small events at bookstores or comic book stores that you arrange with the owner. It's a good idea to invite several creators there at the same time, as you alone are probably not big enough to draw a crowd. But if you offer a wide variety of interesting creators, that will bring in more people and it will give you a chance to meet folks you otherwise wouldn't be able to.

Craft Fairs. These are good for artists, crafts people, and comic creators. Often, you are the only comic selling at a craft fair which either means you'll stand out or be ignored. It can go both ways, but it's usually worth trying out the event at least once.

Screenings. Almost every city has a film presence now, so no matter how large or small it is, they will have events like panels, screenings, and other networking events. Go to them.

Meet-ups. Get online and sign up for local meet-up groups that are tailored to your interests. Use them as an opportunity to make friends and learn more about your craft and your industry. Promotion will come later.

For all of the events, be sure to bring some sort of marketing material with you (i.e., business cards, postcards, etc.). Talk about mutual interests, your project, their project, and make friends. They could be your future backers.

CHAPTER 3.

CRUNCHING THE NUMBERS

This is where you sit down and figure out what everything will cost to produce and deliver your project. You may already know that you need $3,000 to produce your project, but with fees, costs of incentives, etc., that will not and shouldn't be your funding goal. Otherwise, you will lose money. This is one of the hardest things to figure out, and I strongly suggest you put together a spreadsheet to help you accomplish this task. (There is a sample worksheet in the back of this book.)

Questions you need to answer first if you haven't already:

- How much will it cost to produce my project?
- How much will each reward tier cost me, and how much will it generate?
- Have you calculated your shipping costs?
- How much are your mailers going to cost?
- If you are making it yourself, how much will all of the materials cost?
- If you are successful and get lots of backers, is there a place to store the inventory, or will you have to rent out a storage unit? If you need storage, add that cost to your spreadsheet.

Let's run through an example of how much mailing one reward will cost and what is left over to produce your project. Let's start with a $25 reward level. In my case, the physical reward would be one signed comic, plus a bookmark. The weight is 5 ounces, which includes the mailer. Remember that Kickstarter takes 5% as their cut, and Stripe can take anywhere from 3% to 5% in payment processing fees. For simplicity, let's take 10% off the top when doing your spreadsheet.

DOMESTIC EXAMPLE – $25.00 Reward Level (Shipping included in the $25)

A	B	C	D	E	F
Cost of Reward (including bookmark, packaging.)	Kickstarter Fees (5%)	Stripe Fees (5%)	Domestic Shipping	Reward Level	Money available for product creation
$2.25	$0.75	$0.75	$2.69	$25	$18.56

You add columns A , B, C , and D, and then subtract that from column E which gives you $18.56 in column F.

International shipping is tricky and has bitten many a creator's butt. Remember when I said you need to do prototypes of every type of package and figure out how much it costs to mail it to various countries? This is where it pays off in understanding how much money you're really making. At the time I calculated this, $10 was the average shipping cost for Canada, Australia, and Germany (5 oz.). Obviously, if your package weighs more, then you will need to tack on more postage for the backer to pay. I generally don't like to charge more than $24 for international shipping, because anything more than that will dissuade international backers from pledging to your Kickstarter. If the real cost of international postage is over $24, I try to spread the cost out among the other rewards, so I don't hammer the upper reward tiers with exorbitant shipping costs. You will need to take that into account on your spreadsheet if you decide to do it.

Unlike in my previous campaigns, Kickstarter now allows you to select the country you might be shipping to and add appropriate shipping charges if you chose not to average the costs out. I was able to use this method in my last campaign, so I didn't have to average out shipping costs to other countries. And since I know that Endicia.com will give me a slight discount on international shipping, I'm able to charge a bit less to my international backers. I call this a win-win.

INTERNATIONAL EXAMPLE – $25.00 Reward Level (Backer Pays $10 Shipping Charge)

A	B	C	D	E	F
Cost of Reward (includes bookmark, packaging)	Kickstarter Fees (5%)	Stripe Fees (5%)	International Shipping	Reward Level	Money available for product creation
$2.25	$0.75	$0.75	$7.70 (Canada)	$25 + $10	23.55
$2.25	$0.75	$0.75	$11.48 (Australia)	$25 + $10	19.77

Once again, you add columns A, B, C, and D, but this time you subtract the total amount of column E from that amount to determine the total amount of money available for your project in column F.

When you know what money is available to create your product, you'll have a better idea of what your funding goal should be.

CHAPTER 4.

WRITING YOUR KICKSTARTER HOMEPAGE

Before you do anything, get online and set up your account on whichever platform you have decided to use. This can take longer than you think, as you are required to include bank account numbers and other personal information that needs to be verified. I'd suggest setting it up at least two weeks before you intend to launch. That should give you plenty of time to deal with any glitches. The Kickstarter website is very user friendly, but if you are a bit computer-phobic, allow yourself time to go through it and don't think you need to finish it all at once.

I would suggest not having a campaign run longer or shorter than 30 days. The reason being is that any longer will drive you insane and any shorter will not give you breathing room to build momentum if you need it; however, Kickstarter has been experimenting with new programs like "Make 100," where creators focus on editions of 100 limited editions and shorter campaign periods. A similar program still exists where the creator must include a limited reward capped at 100 backers. I have no doubt that they will be introducing other types of projects in the future.

Having done a number of Kickstarter campaigns, I've developed a few pet peeves when looking at other campaigns. Number one on the list is lack of clarity as to what you hope to achieve. In marketing terms, it's referred to as a "Call to Action." Often, I have to search the entire page looking for what the creator is asking for (i.e. fund art and production, print a 200 page graphic novel, etc.). No one has time for that.

No matter which platform you use, the following is what makes a homepage stand out:

- Organization
- Simplicity
- Readability

Let's review what needs to go on your homepage.

Remember I talked about my pet peeve in having to search for what the project was about and what the creators wanted? These first two items should be at the top of your homepage, though the order is up to you. There are exceptions, and I'll show you what those are in the Case Studies Section and why they work in those campaigns.

> **1. Describe in 25 words or less what your story is or what your project is about**. This is the first thing people will read when your little widget box pops on the Kickstarter Preview Page. (We'll call this your "Widget Pitch.") This may take a while to write, so start working on it long before you launch so you can rework it—a lot. These are difficult to do effectively, so don't think you can rush in at the last minute and write something that makes sense.
>
> **2. What is your "Call to Action?"** In other words, what are you going to use the money for if you are fully funded? Make sure you are clear on your goals.
>
> **3. Expand on your story and the project.** This is where you can get into more detail about your characters, world, and

what this project means to you. At this point, you need to make this personal, but not too personal. You are not just selling your project, you are selling yourself. Backers should feel like they know you, like you, and most of all… trust in your sincerity.

4. Your characters. For comic creators, be sure to list your major characters with brief biographies and an image of each of them.

5. Show samples of your work. For comic creators, put up at least six (6) pages of art that are large enough that users can read the lettering. You can certainly add more, especially if special pin-ups are part of your reward tiers. But you need to add enough so that potential backers get a good feel for your work; however, don't add so many that your page goes on forever. For filmmakers, post videos of your work and your cast.

For other types of artists, show samples of not only your work, but possibly your process, as well. Many backers find that to be interesting, and it will set your page apart from others.

6. Biographies of you and your team. It really helps to add short biographies of you and your team along with headshots and links to their websites, awards, other work, etc. (Headshots are nice, but not critical.) This increases your credibility, no matter what you are trying to fund.

7. Why this story or project. Now, I'm not talking specifically about your comic, graphic novel, or whatever type of project you are working on, but there should be themes and elements in your story or project that are important to you. Because that's why you created the project in the first place, right?

What I'm talking about is YOUR story. Many of the creators I've consulted with have a hard time talking about themselves. Like myself, they are introverts who think no one could possibly be interested in them, but on Kickstarter or any type of crowdfunding project, you're not just trying to sell your project to potential backers, you're selling YOURSELF. You may be asking why you should bother doing this. Shouldn't potential backers just be interested in my project? Why should they care about me?

Well, the answer to that is, whether you like it or not, you and your project are linked. And you need to find a way to connect to your backers on an emotional level. To help you discover what that link is, ask yourself the following questions:

- Why did you write this particular story?
- What is your history?
- What are the themes that permeate your story or project?

Here is an example of what I mean that I pulled from my last campaign.

> *I love writing* Boston Metaphysical Society. *Not only does it bring my love of science fiction and history together (which by the way, equals steampunk), the steampunk time period allows me to address the themes of classism, sexism, and racism in America in a thoughtful and entertaining way. For at its very core,* Boston Metaphysical Society *is an American story. And you can't tell an American story without including women and people of color.*

> *It has been and always will be important to me to write characters who, though they come from diverse backgrounds and have different points of view, are able to work together for the common good.*

Boston Metaphysical Society begin as a TV Pilot which I wrote while I was in the MFA Program in Screenwriting at UCLA. It was somewhat inspired by a script I had written called Stargazer, *which was about a real-life astronomer who lived in Boston in the late 1880s. (*Stargazer *went on to win the Sloan Fellowship.) It was suggested that I adapt* Boston Metaphysical *into a six-issue graphic novel mini-series. I agreed and the hunt was on for an artist. Many months later, I met Emily Hu through a mutual friend, and a partnership was born. Her passion for the project matched my own, and I knew the story was in good hands. I launched* Boston Metaphysical Society *as a webcomic in May of 2012. The following year we printed a special edition of the first chapter.*

Through a combination of self-funding and the generous support of Kickstarter backers like you, we were able to finish the six issue series, and now we are back to print this expanded version of the trade.

However, by wading into the deep end of the pool, I discovered a terrible truth – I love writing comics.

So, I bring you Samuel, Caitlin, and Granville who represent the best, the worst, and every shade of gray of the society in which they live. They are products of their world, yet strive for not only more, but better.

Much like you and I.

By backing this project, you would not only be supporting the printing of the trade paperback, but a vision of a future where the teamwork and sacrifice of a diverse group of individuals ultimately defeats evil.

Other excellent examples of the above can be found in *Oh,*

Hell by George Wassil, *Black Suit of Death* by Benjamin Kreger and Edward Ellsworth, and *After the Gold Rush* by Miles Greb.

8. Testimonials. These are quotes from positive reviews from credible sources, not your mom, sister, or a close friend. Be sure to add links to those sources, as well. Testimonials also help establish your credibility.

9. Budget. Include a budget, even if it's a rough one. Many people use a classic pie chart while others simply spell out how much everything will cost.

10. Reward Tiers. Use creative names for each of your reward tiers. For example, you could use the names of your characters or locations within the story. You could also use ones that are self-explanatory, like "Digital Package Only." We will go into more depth about reward tiers in a later section.

11. Stretch Goals. You should know what they are and crunch the numbers before you launch. That way, if you do well, you're not scrambling to figure out what they should be and if you can afford them. Only give physical stretch goals to those who have pledged to a level where they are already receiving a package in the mail that is large enough to include your stretch goals.

For example, if the reward tier for a physical copy of your book is $15 (and includes lower tier rewards), you could decide that your first stretch goal is three stickers. Only those people who have pledged $20 and above will receive those stickers. Not only will they fit easily into the package you had already planned on sending, but they will not add much in postage, if any. (It might also induce those at the $15 level to increase their pledge to $20 just to get the stickers.) Otherwise, you'll be paying additional postage for those who did not pay for it, and the extra postage will eat into your profit margin. Be sure to explain that only those who have pledged over a certain amount will receive whichever stretch goals you decide upon. No need to make backers angry over not getting something they thought they were going to receive.

As an added note, I personally do not like to post what the stretch goals are until we get close or pass the initial funding goal. I think it looks rather presumptuous; however, that's a personal thing, and it's entirely up to you if you want to go ahead and post them when you launch.

11. Risks and Challenges. Tell us your background in fulfillment. Have you ever done a print run before? Have you ever managed a massive amount of mailings? Do you see any problems that you can head off before they become an impediment to fulfillment? Be truthful and sincere.

12. Shipping Damage. As of yet, I have not included a policy that requires the backer to pay for additional shipping charges if the reward is damaged by USPS and you have to send out another one. It is something to consider, though I have not seen anyone else do it and I'm not sure how well it would be received by the Kickstarter community.

All of the above applies to any crowdfunding project on any platform.

Next, we will take a look at some case studies. Because of copyright law, I did not include their artwork; however, you can view them online at Kickstarter.com at any time.

CASE STUDY #1 – AFTER DAYLIGHT

Created by Sarah Roark, *After Daylight* began as a webcomic that went to print when Sarah decided she had enough material to fill a nice bound volume. She was looking for a funding goal of $5,800 and ended up raising $6,344. I worked with Sarah before, during and after her campaign, though I will say her homepage was in very good shape and needed very little tweaking when I reviewed it. Let's first take a look at her "Widget Pitch."

Life is hilarious. Why should Undeath be any different?

In nine words, we learned that this project is a comedy, probably has vampires, and is definitely tongue-in-cheek.

Now, let's take a look at the top of her page below the video.

"an awesome, sassy vampire webcomic...with unique and fresh ideas"
— Meg Markey, ReadComicBooks.net
"shows surprising depth quickly"
— Chuck Wendig, author of the Miriam Black books and the Heartland series

It's that time! **After Daylight**, *your one-stop shop for satirical vampire comedy/drama with a splash of socially-aware snark (okay, maybe more than a splash) has been updating faithfully as a weekly webcomic since August of 2012. Now 100 hand-shaded pages are in the can, the grand plot arc of the first "season" is all wrapped up, and it's time for it to sail out into the world in gorgeous print.*

As you can see, Sarah placed her testimonials at the top. This works very well in this case, because the quotes are short and to the point. Then, she clearly explains what the comic is about, that it is a webcomic, and that her goal is to take "100 hand-shaded pages" and put them into print. Now you know exactly what this project is about, and you haven't even read a quarter of a page. If you're interested in the project, you'll read on.

Next, she expands on the story and tells you about her point of view on vampires. We, as potential backers, now get an overview of the project, and even better, we learn a little bit more about Sarah. We know she's funny, sarcastic, and clearly has fun with her project, which makes us want to have fun, too!

Great. So what's After Daylight?

Well, you gotta understand. I've been writing vampire fiction on a professional basis since the late 90's, and I still love the bloodthirsty little dears to death, but I can only take them so seriously anymore. As an author, I love the juiciness of a setting where humans must share the planet (or not) with other sentient, powerful beings. Who drink blood. But as a fan, I've gotten so tired of books and shows that drop all these intriguing hints about how that setting would work...aaaand then end up way too busy destroying the protagonists' romance for the fourth time to really follow up on it. Not naming any names.

So I've taken that premise of "humans discover vampires! En masse!" and put my own tongue-mostly-in-cheek twist on it. And I've written in all those bloodsuckers I knew had to exist if there really were bloodsuckers, but for some reason we never see them. You know: the ones too busy working a crappy night job to stand around with perfect hair, moping existentially. The ones who think blood bank discards taste like rusty nails. The ones who listen to a little too much talk radio. The ones who actually reflect the incredible variety of a modern urban population. The ones who're more scared of mortals than the mortals are of them.

In the next section she's added art and short biographies of her characters to give us a better sense of her art style and who the characters are.

> *We see much of this through the eyes of one "Cat" Bernstein, ex-folk-rocker turned undead retail drudge, but this series is all about strong ensemble cast. No matter what kind of vamps you like, I've probably got one for you! Volume 1 takes us through the ominous creeping dawn of Daylight — that's the vampires' unhappy nickname for this revelation — from its first deniable Internet leaks (and the inevitable LOLmacros) to the full monty of the inescapable spotlight.*

> *Let's just say, hijinks ensue. But don't take my word for it. Feel free to browse over to the webcomic at http://www.afterdaylight.com and take a look!*

Sarah follows with a more in-depth explanation of the project, why you should pledge, and some of its history.

> *Okay, but why should I back this if the webcomic is free? Glad you asked.*

> ***Reason #1: The book is way cooler.*** *It's bigger and much higher-resolution, so even if you're reading the PDF, you'll enjoy a nicer view of the lovingly-detailed art and all the jokey little Easter eggs. The print edition will be even lovelier, what with its hip, graphic, UV-spot-coated cover design and all. Both print and PDF versions will have some material not available on the website — with possibly even more bonus goodies, if we can hit stretch goals! Finally, while* After Daylight *works fine as a page-a-week fix because of the comedy, it also has a continuing dramatic plot that's more satisfying to read in extended bursts. The book/e-book format makes those leisurely reading sessions much more convenient and pleasurable.*

> ***Reason #2: Creators gotta eat.*** *We live in exciting times.*

Crowdfunding platforms like Kickstarter are opening up whole new possibilities for indie comics. Webcomics in particular have eagerly added it to the business model that's been emerging over the last decade or so – a model in which you can make it even if your stories are too wild and weird, too niche, too unconventional in art style, or too "hard to market" to sell to risk-averse major publishers. I've spent the last two years basically doing my "ante up" – proving to myself that I can meet a regular deadline while creating a story and characters that make people laugh, think, and care. I believe the reader response so far has borne this out. But a comic like this is time- and labor-intensive to produce, and rent still comes annoyingly due every month. So now I have to verify that I can make at least enough money at this to be able to continue with the series. Your pledge money is funding an honest-to-goodness professional offset print run, but this is an all-or-nothing deal. If the funding goal isn't met by the deadline, no money changes hands and that means I can't buy the run, so I need the help of each and every one of you with pledging and spreading the word.

But if we succeed, I can print enough premium-quality books not only to reward my backers, but also to sell on an ongoing basis at conventions, through small retailers, and on the Internet. In other words, your Kickstarter support can help make my indie creative career viable in a way that simply wouldn't have been possible twenty years ago. As a child of the pre-Web era, I find this change amazing! I hope you do too.

All right, you've sold me. Now tell me what goodies I get!

She then adds a visual breakdown of some of the rewards, as well as the stretch goals. I'd like to note that Sarah did not post the stretch goals at the start of her campaign. It was only after she had gotten close and eventually achieved those goals that she revealed them.

I have many pledge levels for you — take a look on the right. In all likelihood, there's one that suits your desires and budget. (If not, contact me — some customization of pledges is certainly available!) But just to give you an idea, here's some of what's on offer at different tiers:

+ **Immortality!** *If by "immortality" you're willing to take "a thank-you by name in the historic first edition!"*

+ **After Daylight, Vol 1– premium softcover and/or PDF edition**, *with possible further upgrades in stretch goals (over 100 pages of story)!*

+ *Yer very own button, featuring Cat's cheery lovable puss!*

+ *A "SO. Not. An Early Riser." greeting card for all occasions!*

+ *A Kickstarter-exclusive 8×10 giclee art print on premium watercolor paper!*

+ *11×17 giclee art prints of Vol. 1 pages (with or without text)!*

+ *A making-of PDF with concept art and creation notes!*

+ *Custom art creations*

+ *And more!*

STRETCH GOALS

$6300 (NOW IN PLAY)
Added material and guest art for the book — including but not limited to the making-of PDF pages
Surprise bonus physical reward!

$6800 (Locked)
Detailed sneak peek at Vol. 2
Surprise bonus physical reward!

$7300 (Locked)
This coffin may open a crack as the goal approaches...

Sarah has made even the unknown stretch goals fun and humorous, which keeps it nicely consistent with the entire tone of the project. Now, let's take a look at her "Risks and Challenges" section.

+ The 100 full comic pages and 5 minicomics that make up Volume 1 are already completed, so apart from layout — which is currently in progress — the book is finished. This has already been a multi-year labor, which I'm very proud and happy to have invested in.

+ There can be no collaboration problems because After Daylight is a one-woman shop. My boss may be a taskmaster, but she can't fire me! Yes, if I get run over by a truck or something, then no further volumes will be created — and while the first big plot arc is finished in Vol. 1, I plan many more wicked plot arcs that do need me to keep making them. So I hope you'll join me in my fervent desire that no trucks engage me in any right-of-way disputes.

+ This is a first Kickstarter. I've crunched oh, so many spreadsheet numbers and lined up multiple potential vendors for this, but it's still always possible that something will happen to cause a production delay beyond those already anticipated (for instance, my most likely print vendor ships from overseas, so that multi-week delay is all but certain). I'll be very clear about what I expect for turnaround times on each reward category once the funding goal is reached and fulfillment begins. If it looks like there'll be a hiccup, delay, or need to switch vendors, I'll keep everyone apprised of those developments as they happen and listen carefully to backer feedback.

+ In planning this campaign, I'm lucky to follow a path already trodden by similar bound-volume projects that have funded successfully, and whose fulfillment phases were much like what I'm planning. Their triumphs and agonies have been my teachers. I've been soliciting advice from multiple colleagues for many months now, and as a result, I believe I've built in reasonable cushions and contingencies for the known problems of crowdfunding a graphic novel. (For instance, NOT forgetting shipping expenses and fees!) Again, however, if something unanticipated comes up that has the potential to affect my backers, frequent and informative updates will be my response.

+ If I have my way, After Daylight *will be around for many years to come — so my long-term relationship with my readers is one of the most important things in the world to me. In all I do with this campaign, the desire to keep that relationship going strong is my guide.*

Sarah was extremely thorough in this section. I personally thought she could have edited it down a bit, but kudos to her for not holding back and giving you the unvarnished truth.

When you take a look at her page on Kickstarter.com, you will notice her art is well organized throughout the page. Also, you will see that she added updates to the top of her page. Her original project starts at the testimonials.

CASE STUDY #2 – *Zombie Boy* by Mark Stokes

Zombie Boy is a very cute, all-ages comic strip that Mark has been drawing for over twenty years. It was definitely time for him to put them into a bound volume. I worked with Mark before, during, and after the campaign to prepare him for one of the most stressful things he would do in his life. He worked and re-worked the homepage and the reward tiers until they rocked.

Mark was looking for a funding goal of $6,800, and he ultimately raised $7,234.

Here is his "Widget Pitch:"

> Zombie Boy Comics: *Some Kind of Horrible collects the first 200* Zombie Boy *comic strips by award-winning cartoonist Mark Stokes.*

In twenty-one words, Mark has told us who he is, and his goal, and you know with a title like *Zombie Boy*, it has to be humorous. In the next section, Mark describes the project and the story a little more.

> Zombie Boy Comics *follows the afterlife and times of "living challenged" Morgan McCorkindale, a.k.a. Zombie Boy, and his pals Duncan, Beatrice, Claustria, Boog and Solstice. It posts three times a week at zombieboycomics.com. The strip has been posting online since August, 2010. The purpose of this Kickstarter is to collect the first 200* Zombie Boy *comic strips into a softcover book for the first time ever!*

Mark then adds three pages from the comic strip which highlight the main character of the story before he tells us about the Kickstarter exclusives. (A "Kickstarter Exclusive" is a reward that can only be received by pledging to the Kickstarter. You will not be able to buy them later. This is often used as an incentive to get people to pledge.)

> *KICKSTARTER EXCLUSIVES include a custom bookmark, a custom postcard, a custom made vinyl* Zombie Boy *sticker, an* ORIGINAL ZOMBIE BOY COMIC BOOK, *original sketches and illustrations*, ORIGINAL ZOMBIE BOY COMIC STRIP ART *and* GUEST APPEARANCES IN A ZOMBIE BOY COMIC STRIP, *with optional animated versions!*

He uses colorful and fun illustrations of each reward level to make it easier on the potential backers to figure out what they can't live without. Mark does the same thing with his stretch goals.

Now, for those of you who are Photoshop-challenged like me, it's perfectly fine to write out your rewards and stretch goals. I know I did, and I'll show that to you in the next case study.

As for Mark's "Risks and Challenges" section, he keeps it short, sweet, and to the point.

> *I've successfully published three comic books and have done pre-production on numerous print projects over the years. All the interior book art is completed, so it is mostly going to be prepping this work for print. Risks could occur either in printing delays or in the custom art involved with the Rewards. Should any delay occur at any point, you will be promptly informed.*

CASE STUDY #3 – *Boston Metaphysical Society*

Using my third Kickstarter as an example, I was able to pare down my elevator pitch to suit my "Widget Pitch."

> *An ex-Pinkerton detective and his spirit photographer partner battle supernatural forces in late 1800s Boston. (six-issue mini-series)*

At the top of the page, I wanted to be sure and thank Scott Baker, who created the video, and Reference Recordings, who graciously allowed us to use their music on the video. I felt it was important to acknowledge what they had done immediately since it was so important to the project. Then, I stated the "Call to Action" and posted the Geekie Award nomination in what amounts to a testimonial.

> *A special thank you to Reference Recordings for use of portions*

of the Bruckner Symphony Number 9, "Tutti" CD and a BIG THANK YOU to Scott Baker (4scottbaker@gmail.com) for making this video.

Boston Metaphysical Society *is A SIX-ISSUE CREATOR-OWNED STEAMPUNK SUPERNATURAL MINI-SERIES.*

Nominated for Best Comic/Graphic Novel at the 2014 GEEKIE AWARDS.

Boston Metaphysical Society *needs your help to produce and print the fifth chapter in our six-issue mini-series.*

In the next section, I delved deeper into the storyline, which segued into introducing the characters along with using their images.

The year is 1895... An evil from a parallel dimension escaped and now roams the city of Boston. Faced with a new century and new steam technology, the social and political status quo is turned on its head. People are uncomfortable with change and, in fact, many people fear it. That fear and the violence which follows cause a psychic rift to puncture the veil of space and time allowing the entity known as "The Shifter" to escape. Feeding on the resentment and fear between the rich and poor, "The Shifter" triggers a rash of murders. Four of the greatest minds of the time have banded together to try and stop this malevolent entity. Known only as B.E.T.H., they are:

Images from the comic of Bell, Edison, Tesla, and Houdini

THEY FAIL.

Against their better judgment, they look to a man driven by revenge – SAMUEL HUNTER.

Image of Samuel Hunter

For the one mistake The Shifter made was killing Samuel's wife. An ex-Pinkerton detective, Samuel gathers his unlikely team of... Caitlin O'Sullivan, Medium and Spirit Photographer:

Image of Caitlin O'Sullivan

and Granville Woods, Scientist Extraordinaire:

Image of Granville Woods

They are the Boston Metaphysical Society.

I then show four sample pages of the comic and talk more about the project.

Boston Metaphysical Society *is written by Madeleine Holly-Rosing and drawn by Emily Hu.*

My husband and I believe in this project so much that we have spent our own money to complete the series, but our pocket book is not infinite so we need your help to produce and print chapter five (24 pages, which includes 2 pages of bonus material).

Where the money goes...Your backing would enable us to pay for art production, coloring, printing enough copies of chapter five to send off to backers with some leftover to sell at conventions, incentives, shipping (which includes mailing envelopes/tubes, postage and handling.) And, of course, the Amazon fees (5% off the top, plus credit card fees.)

All printing is done by Prestige Printers in their plant in Houston, TX.

(Note: Where you print is important to some people, as they like to see printing based in the U.S. whenever economically possible.)

Unlike Mark and Sarah who write and draw their own comics,

my drawing is pretty much stick figures, so I had to hire an artist, colorist, and a letterer, among others. If you're a writer/creator like myself, then this is the place to put in the short biographies of you and your team.

THE TEAM:

Madeleine Holly-Rosing – *Writer/Creator: A TV and feature film writer, Madeleine holds an MFA in Screenwriting from UCLA, where she won numerous awards as well as the Sloan Fellowship. Madeleine has published a number of short stories and novellas based on the* Boston Metaphysical Society *universe. Formerly a nationally ranked epee fencer, she has competed nationally and internationally. She is an avid reader of science fiction, steampunk, fantasy, and historical military fiction.*

Emily Hu – *Artist: Emily is a graduate from the School of Visual Arts in New York City. She has been drawing ever since she was little, and it's been her lifelong dream to make it as a comic book artist. Her main influences are Eduardo Risso, Becky Cloonan, and Ito Junji. She works freelance and has created covers for BOOM!* Boston Metaphysical Society *universe. Formerly a nationally ranked epee fencer, she has competed nationally and internationally. She is an avid reader of science fiction, steampunk, fantasy and historical military fiction. is her first comic book series.*

Gloria Caeli – *Colorist: Based in Jakarta, she has worked for Avicom Advertising and Stellar Labs. Her most recent projects are* Boston Metaphysical Society *universe. Formerly a nationally ranked epee fencer, she has competed nationally and internationally. She is an avid reader of science fiction, steampunk, fantasy and historical military fiction. and* Voodoo. *She, like anyone else, enjoys music, photography, travelling, and reads a lot of genre-related books.*

Fahriza Kamaputra – *Colorist: Based in Jakarta, Fahriza is a self-taught comics and concept artist. He worked as a colorist on* Vienetta and The Stupid Aliens *which led to his work on the webcomic,* Rokki *with Stellar Labs.*

Troy Peteri – *Letterer (Chapters 1-3): Troy is a Los Angeles based letterer whose credits include* Amazing Spider-Man, Iron Man, *and roughly 98% of all the comics from Top Cow Productions for the last 6+ years. He also co-wrote and lettered* Abattoir, *a miniseries for Radical Comics.*

Shawn Aldridge – *Letterer (Chapter 4) is a Portland-based writer and letterer. He's best known for his awarding-winning creator-owned sci-pulp series,* Vic Boone. *He also writes and co-created* GoGetters *from MonkeyBrain with artist Christopher Peterson. His work has also appeared in* FUBAR, *the NYT bestselling anthology series.*

I added a picture of the cover art for chapter 4 and then the testimonials.

Boston Metaphysical *is one of my favorite webcomics not just because I'm a sucker for any comics that feature Harry Houdini in lead roles (though I am) or because I love comics that use ghosts in different ways than most strips do (though I am). No,* Boston Metaphysical *is one of my favorite webcomics, because Madeleine Holly-Rosing creates a wonderful fictional world with bold characters and thoroughly entertaining plots. And because of Houdini and the ghosts. I like ghosts. -Jason Sacks, Publisher, Comics Bulletin www.comicsbulletin.com*

With over <cough, cough> years in the comic business as a writer, editor, artist, and a publisher, I've worked with many new and established talented writers and artists. Madeleine Holly-Rosing and Emily Hu are the real deal. It's hard to believe that Boston Metaphysical Society *is their first comic book series. With its* *spot-on writing and elegant illustrations, it's got something that crosses over genres and refuses to be pigeon-holed. We'll see more of this dynamic duo. Back this Kickstarter with me and you'll be able to boast you knew them when, as well. – Dave Elliott, A1/Atomeka Press*

The Boston Metaphysical Society *has more diversity in a story set over 100 years ago in Boston than most modern-day stories in New York City do. That alone should let you know this series is different in a great way. If the idea of Tesla, monsters made of magnets, or spirit photographers intrigue you, you should be supporting this series. – Dr. Alexander Bustos, Comic Attack*

As a huge fan of steampunk, I was very happy to be introduced to the webcomic, Boston Metaphysical Society. *Ms. Holly-Rosing nails the tone with her expert writing, and her artist, Ms. Hu, is a wonder. I definitely want to see how this story ends and will be backing this Kickstarter. (As you should, too.) – Bryn Pryor (Writer/Director, Cowboys and Engines)*

I actually have more quotes than this, and you may too, but don't overdo it. Everyone will get the point by quickly scanning who wrote them.

Remember I mentioned my lack of Photoshop skills? This is how I solved it for the reward tiers.

Incentives:

Our incentives not only include the print version of Chapter 5 and an expanded pdf version, but also a BMS bookmark, short stories, A BRAND NEW BMS NOVELLA, fan art in the various PDF packages, and wait for it...

THE NEW BOSTON METAPHYSICAL SOCIETY NIKOLA TESLA LAPEL PIN DESIGNED BY EMILY HU! *(Pin is one* *inch in diameter, antique brass with standard military clasp in the back.)*

I inserted a photo of the pin here.

Depending on the package you pick, we have fan art not only from ANA KING, but CALVIN GARCIA, as well.

I inserted the pictures of their fan art here.

My stretch goals were pretty simple for this campaign.

STRETCH GOALS:

STRETCH GOAL #1: $8,350.00
TESLA STICKERS!
The stickers are 3 inches in diameter and printed on dull gold foil paper to give it that steamy look. [You must have pledged the Granville Woods $20 package or higher to receive the stickers. Min. of three (3) stickers per backer.]
(Sample Image)

STRETCH GOAL #2: LOCKED

My "Risks and Challenges" section was straightforward for the third Kickstarter.

In order to continue to produce the quality comic you have come to expect in the shortest amount of time possible, we need to ask for a little more money than we did in the last Kickstarter. I successfully delivered all of the rewards from our last Kickstarter and managed five successful print runs of the comic (1st Chapter Special Edition; 1st chapter – 24-page edition; 2nd chapter – 24-page edition; chapter 3 – 28-page edition; and chapter 4 – 24-page edition). I have also been handling fulfillment through my own website store for over two years. I do not anticipate any problems; however, if there are any production delays or hiccups with the printer, you'll be the first to know.

You'll note how different it is from my second Kickstarter, since the circumstances were different having re-launched from a failed campaign.

We learned a lot from our last Kickstarter, so my husband and I decided that we would fund the art production for the rest of the issues in the six-issue mini-series and use Kickstarter as a way for backers to pre-order each issue as they become available. That way we can scale back the goal substantially and have a far greater chance of achieving it.

Since I have managed three successful print runs of the comic (1st Chapter Special Edition; 1st chapter – 24-page edition and 2nd chapter – 24-page edition) and I have been handling fulfillment through my own website store for over a year, I do not anticipate any problems; however, if there are any production delays or hiccups with the printer, you'll be the first to know.

OTHER CAMPAIGNS TO STUDY

I'd also suggest studying the following campaigns for reward tier ideas, how they structure their page and updates, as well as general best practices.

For Comics:

Skies of Fire by Ray Chou and Vincenzo Ferriero (Kickstarter)

Salvagers and *Shelter Division* by Bob Salley (Kickstarter)

Ichabod Jones: Monster Hunter by Russell Nohelty (Kickstarter)

For Film:

5th Passenger by Scott Baker and Morgan Lariah (Kickstarter)

Iron by Semara Lerman (Seed&Spark)

Real Artists by Cameo Wood (Seed&Spark)

For Anthologies:

Steampunk World and *Steampunk Universe* by Steven Saus (Kickstarter)

Monsters and other Scary Shit by Russell Nohelty (Kickstarter)

The Sea is Ours by Jaymee Goh (editor) (Indiegogo)

Holdfast Anthology by Laurel Sills (Indiegogo)

Next, we'll talk about the video.

CHAPTER 5.

DEVELOPING YOUR VIDEO

"Why do I have to make a video? Can't they just read my page?" Good questions, but I'll let you in on a little secret—not everyone is going to read your page, nor is everyone going to watch your video. The reason is that some people are visual and others are not. I rarely watch the video, even if I like the project. There is also the pesky problem of expectation. As crowdfunding has evolved, a video has become mandatory to the process. To not have one makes you look unprofessional.

There are many ways to shoot your video: web cam, green screen, animation software, etc. How you pull it together will depend on time, money, and experience level. I was fortunate to have a friend who is not only an indie director and steady-cam operator, but has a green screen in his apartment and the software to create and edit a video. If you are not so fortunate, there is nothing wrong with using a web cam at home, but be sure there is nothing embarrassing in the background.

Here are the basic requirements:

- Introduce yourself.
- Pitch your story.
- Tell your audience what the money is for ("Call to Action").
- Show samples of your work.

- Keep it under 3 minutes.
- Doesn't have to be perfect, but you must be sincere.

Notice that your video has many of the same requirements as your Kickstarter homepage, but this time you must convey the same basic information in under three minutes.

This would be a good time to get online and take a look at Sarah Roark's *After Daylight* video.

You'll notice she uses a webcam for the "talking head" portion of her video, and behind her are mockups of her book and samples of her art. She introduces herself and her project, then goes into the animated portion, with a voiceover telling us more about it in under three minutes. You can tell she has fun and the project is very much tongue-in-cheek. If it fits the tone of your project, don't be afraid to smile and have a little fun. It will make you appear human and more likable.

Now, let's take a look at *Misfortune High* by Jules Rivera.

We never see Jules except in a photo, but she does the voiceover. It doesn't take long for us to understand what the story is about, what she's asking for, and a little background on her, all while seeing the art from her comic. It's a very tight video that you would do well to emulate if it fits your project.

Zombie Boy by Mark Stokes also takes a fun and light look at his project. It gets to the point quickly and smoothly, and we see Mark talking as well as in some still photos. I really liked the way he demonstrated his process. Mark used iMovie to put together his video.

You are always welcome to take a look at the videos I did for *Boston Metaphysical Society*. Mine is structured differently due to time and economic constraints. The first 30 seconds is me introducing myself and the project, then I tell you what I am asking for (i.e., print of chapter three, etc.). You see the covers of the current issues at the time while I talk. When I finish, it goes into the video that describes the story in more detail and ends with the "Call to Action." We split it up this way so I could use the same video for future Kickstarters (with some minor tweaking) and only have to redo my speaking part.

Other types of software you can use for your video are Motion in Final Cut Pro, Adobe Premiere and After Effects.

MUSIC

Searching for the right music for your video can be time consuming and potentially costly. I wanted to find something that was written in the late 1800s so as to match the theme of my comic. Lucky for me, my husband is an audiophile, and after some research and going through about a dozen CDs, I settled on a piece from Bruckner. He was able to reach out through a friend and contact Reference Recording, who recorded that particular piece. Though the music was in the public domain, we wanted to do the right thing. We asked them how much it would cost to license the music for the video. If it was too costly, we had already decided to use something free. Fortunately for us, they liked the project and gave us permission to use it for the Kickstarter video.

Not everyone is going to be so lucky.

Prior to getting their permission, I spent a lot of time listening to free public domain music on:

Musopen at https://musopen.org/

FreePD at http://freepd.com/

Public Domain Music: 12 Free Online Sources at

http://websearch.about.com/od/publicdomain/tp/Public-Domain-Music.htm

Before you even start looking, be sure to have a sense of what type of music you are looking for (i.e., jazz, classical, techno, etc. It will save you time and lots of headaches).

CHAPTER 6.

REWARD TIERS

Figuring out reward tiers can be a little daunting. There are the obvious ones, like that thing you're actually running the Kickstarter to produce, and then there are all the little things to make the upper reward tiers more inviting. But let's start with the basics... what are you going to name each tier?

If you are producing a comic, film, or book, I'd suggest using the names of your characters or the locations where the story takes place. If you are doing an album, it could be names related to the theme of the CD or musical notes, for instance. Whatever you're doing, just be creative and fun. You don't want to be the person who names their rewards, Reward #1, Reward #2, etc. That's just plain boring.

Each reward tier has a perceived value. Most backers don't mind paying a little more for a Kickstarter reward than what they would pay in the store, because they know it's all going to the project. For example, if your goal is to produce a 200-page softbound printed graphic novel, most backers are willing to pay $25 to $30 for that. This level would also include any lower rewards like bookmarks, digital copies, and a "thank you" on your website; however, you don't want to be charging $50 for the same thing unless you're adding something else of value, like a print, additional digital media, and other items. Your physical rewards may start at around $10 depending on the cost of the reward, packaging, and domestic shipping.

Remember, you have to give your backers value for their money.

As I mentioned before, the average pledge is $25. I refer to this reward tier as your "bread and butter" tier. That means this is the tier where you will receive the most pledges, so make sure it is worth it to the backer. I once saw a campaign where the first physical reward tier started at $100. Not a good idea. Backers really expect to hold something in their hands at the $20 mark, if not less.

Sample Reward Tiers:

- *$5 reward*
- **The Red-Eyed Demon Package***: A digital copy of Chapter Five and a thank you on the website.*
- *Estimated delivery: Dec 2014*

- *$10 reward*
- **The Duncan the Ghost Package***: A digital copy and an unsigned print copy of Chapter Five. A thank you on the website.*
- *Estimated delivery: Jan 2015*
- *Ships anywhere in the world*

- *$15 reward*
- **The Jonathan Weldsmore Package***: A digital copy and print copy of Chapter Five signed by the creator, a BMS bookmark, and a thank you on the website.*
- *Estimated delivery: Jan 2015*
- *Ships anywhere in the world*

- *$15 reward*
- **Digital Package Only***: A digital copy of Chapters One-Five. Chapters One-Four to be delivered two weeks upon successful completion of the campaign and a thank you on the website.*

Chapter Five to be delivered in Dec. 2014.
• *Estimated delivery: Jan 2015*

You should also keep one or two reward tiers in reserve; that way, when you are about two weeks into the campaign, you can announce a "New Reward Level." Post this as an update to your backers, as well as tweeting and posting elsewhere. If you add a really cool tier at, say, the $65 level, it might encourage those at the $50 level and below to increase their pledge. But what this really does is keep your campaign fresh and alive.

Halfway through my third Kickstarter, I added two new rewards: "The Awesome Steampunk Ring One-Book Package" and "The Awesome Steampunk Ring Five-Book Package." Prior to launching, I had arranged to purchase the rings through a friend of mine who makes steampunk jewelry and is widely known throughout the steampunk community. This new reward tier allowed me to address the steampunk community and possibly introduce my comic to those who had not heard about it before.

I sold out of both tiers. This is also a lesson in knowing your market.

These tiers were "limited" in that I only had a limited amount of these particular items for backers to pledge to. When you start filling in the reward section in your Kickstarter account, you will see a field asking you if you wish to limit the reward or not. You can limit any tier you wish, as well as how long it is available. This works well for "Early Bird" rewards. Most campaigns use "Early Bird" rewards as an enticement to get previous backers on board and to help boost the amount of pledges during the critical first three days of launching your campaign.

The reward form will also ask if this reward can be shipped worldwide. Once again, that is up to you, but if you choose to make it available outside the United States or your country of origin, be sure to add the right amount of postage. (See section on "Postage and Mailing.")

Also, be realistic on your delivery date. Most backers are pretty forgiving if you are a month or two late, but don't promise something you can't deliver.

I've said this before, but it's worth repeating that it is always a good idea to research other successful Kickstarters that are similar to your own and take a look at their reward tiers to help give you more ideas.

ADD-ONS

Add-ons are physical rewards that backers can chose to "add on" to their pledge level. Examples would be T-shirts, art prints, additional books, etc. I don't recommend doing them if this is your first Kickstarter, because:

> 1. You have to figure out the domestic and international postage for each item and make sure you post it and collect it.
> 2. You have to note who gets what and not screw it up.

The few exceptions would be:

> 1. If your campaign does exceedingly well and you need to add more items to bring in more backers.
> 2. You're really good at managing a lot of extra inventory.

This is also assuming you are not using a software called Backer Kit, which helps to organize and streamline your campaign. More on that later.

EXCLUSIVES

I briefly mentioned exclusives earlier, but I thought it worth mentioning again. Backers love exclusives. Remember, these are items that will only be available by backing the Kickstarter. You cannot sell them at conventions or elsewhere afterwards. (I suppose you could, but if a backer saw it and posted on social media, you would look bad.)

If your budget allows for exclusives—go for it.

CHAPTER 7.

POSTAGE AND MAILING

You might be wondering why a chapter on postage is not part of the chapter on fulfillment. I can answer that in one word: budget. Be sure you know your mailing costs before you launch and work them into your spreadsheet.

It is <u>imperative</u> that you create prototypes of all packages, weigh them, and then plug in the numbers at USPS.com in order to find out how much they will really cost. Do not guess! You will be wrong. And you will need those numbers to help figure out how much you should be charging at each reward level.

To impress upon you how important it is to do prototype packages and pre-weigh them, let me tell you a story...

I met a man while I was on a panel about Kickstarter campaigns while attending a small steampunk convention. He told me that he was currently running a campaign for a device he had invented and had not realized until after he had launched that he had grossly underestimated the cost of international shipping. He told his backers what he had done and asked that they either 1. add additional money for the postage or 2. remove their pledge and re-pledge with the proper amount of postage.

Unfortunately, his backers fled like the proverbial lemmings and his campaign took a nosedive as people withdrew their pledges, but did not re-pledge. I do not know if he recouped from this disaster and was ultimately successful, but you can imagine how disheartening and stressful that was even if he did manage to make his goal.

On Kickstarter, you can now enter the cost of postage for each individual country. I find that it is easier to just enter it for U.S. and Canada and then the "Anywhere else in the world" category. When I do that, I take my prototype, weigh it and then look it up on USPS for Canada and note it. I then look it up for Australia and Germany. Both those countries are usually very close in cost, and I enter that amount in the "Anywhere in the world" field.

However, if you want to average it and put that number in the "Anywhere in the world" field, I'd suggest averaging (if you are based in the U.S.) the postage of the following countries: Canada, Australia, and Germany. That is how much you will charge your international backers at that particular reward level. Other reward levels may cost a lot more in international postage, but you don't want the cost to be so prohibitive that it scares off international backers. If you choose to keep those reward levels, you can spread the cost around to lower tiers if need be, though I try and avoid that.

There are three types of postage you need to know about:

Media Mail: Everyone uses media mail for their comics as it is the cheapest; however, there is some dispute as to whether or not comics are allowed to use Media Mail by USPS. If you look at Notice 121, dated Oct. 2012, it states, *"Media Mail packages may not contain advertising. Comic books do not meet this standard. Books may contain incidental announcements of other books and sound recordings may contain incidental announcements of other sound recordings."* I interpret this to mean that if your comic books do <u>NOT</u> contain advertising, then they are eligible for Media Mail. (Note: Some of you might fulfill through KaBlam or Greko

Printing and they give you the option to add advertising to decrease your page cost.) I have personally mailed out over a thousand packages by Media Mail that have contained single issues, prints, and the trade paperback and I have never had a problem using Media Mail except for when packages are lost or destroyed as there is no option for insurance. However, none of my books have contained advertising.

If you want to look at what USPS says on their website, they still have an old page up about Media Mail, dated 2008, and Notice 170 Retail Mail Media Mail and Library Mail (no date) which makes no reference to comic books, but references the "no advertising" stipulation. These pages often come up first in a Google search, so keep poking around to find the 2012 page.

Please be aware that USPS has the right to inspect your packages if they are sent by Media Mail, and they have been known to destroy things in the process which is why sometimes it's better to use...

First-Class Parcel: I love First-Class Parcel. If your large envelope is under 5 ounces, it will be cheaper than media mail and it will not be inspected. If over 5 ounces, it can be about a dollar more. The caveat is that the package must weigh under 16 ounces. This is perfect for small items like pins, keychains, buttons, etc.

International First Class Mail: Keep all international packages under 4 pounds or else the cost will quadruple. I am not kidding!

There is always First-Class and Priority Mail, but those can be cost prohibitive. The caveat here is that if you have a number of small, yet bulky, items to ship, the flat-rate boxes might be your best deal. Like I said before, weigh all your items in a variety of different boxes to see where you can save money.

Be aware that as time goes on, postage rates will change which leads me to...

BUYING POSTAGE

I strongly recommend using an online service like Stamps.com or Endicia.com. The reason being is that you can no longer obtain international commercial-based pricing through USPS.com and you will save a significant amount of money on overseas postage if you have over ten international backers. Both have a free, month-long trial, and you can buy media mail and First-Class Parcel postage through their website. Be aware that they require you to enter the backer's phone number for international mailing, so be sure to capture that information when sending out your surveys. Depending on how many backers you have, you might want to invest in a thermal printer for the labels. That way you can print them out, put them on the package, and drop them off at the post office without having to wait in line or annoy the clerks. Or, you can print out international postage on your computer, then tape the label/customs form to the envelope/package with clear packing tape.

PACKAGING

I've used several different types of packaging and been happy with all of them so far. They were:

- Uline Self-Seal White Stay Flats
- Uline Kraft Self-Seal Stay Flats
- Uline Kraft and Poly Self-Seal Bubble Mailers
- Paper Mart Brand Air Bubble Mailers
- Paper Mart Brand Standard Cardboard Boxes
- Paper Mart Brand Mailing Tubes and Top Tuck Mailing Boxes

I also bag my comics and sometimes board them depending on where they are going. Longer trips=stronger mailer.

Also, be sure to put clear tape over the lapels, as the USPS tends to shred them if they run it through the sorter.

SUPPLIERS

With locations nationwide, Uline is one of the biggest retailers of shipping supplies and has an extensive inventory and selection. They can also be pretty pricey. I've branched out and started using eBay and also Paper Mart in Orange, CA. Paper Mart does not have the selection that Uline does, but I found it has generally been cheaper (with a few exceptions) and the quality is the same. Obviously, there are other suppliers out there, but these are the ones I have dealt with.

CHAPTER 8.

WRITING A PRESS RELEASE

Press releases are part of what is commonly called an Electronic Press Kit (EPK). For those of you unfamiliar with the term, an EPK includes contact information, a short biography of you and/ or your team members, samples and/or links to your work, positive quotes from real reviews and links back to their websites, links to any press coverage, social media links, any upcoming events, and an up-to-date press release. Before you launch, you should put an EPK together.

A press release can be about a new project, a new team member that's come on board – for example, a new artist or colorist – and, of course, your Kickstarter. You need to look for an angle that makes your press release stand out from others, especially since there are so many other Kickstarters out there begging for attention. You also want to think about writing it for your audience, and remember to send along links to your Kickstarter and your website. If you refer to a review within the body of the press release, be sure to include a link to that as well. And don't forget to send along photos, art, and any relevant videos.

If it is not stated on the reporter's or news outlet's website, be sure to ask if they prefer press releases to be sent as an attachment or in the body of the email.

Below is a sample press release that I wrote for my first Kickstarter. Notice the news angle I took to grab the reader's attention.

SAMPLE PRESS RELEASE #1

Boston Metaphysical Society Webcomic

FOR IMMEDIATE RELEASE

Contact: Madeleine Holly-Rosing
Phone: (XXX) XXX-XXXX
Email: bostonmetaphysical@gmail.com

BOSTON METAPHYSICAL SOCIETY LAUNCHES KICKSTARTER
Steampunk Webcomic Looks to Inject More Diversity into Comics

BURBANK, CA. Madeleine Holly-Rosing, writer/creator of the steampunk webcomic, *Boston Metaphysical Society,* announced she would be launching a Kickstarter campaign on Wednesday, October 16th, to finish the last three issues in the six-issue mini-series. "I always finish what I start," Ms. Holly-Rosing commented, "so I'm reaching out to our fans to help complete this story arc."

The story is about an ex-Pinkerton detective, his spirit photographer partner, and a genius scientist who battle supernatural forces in late 1800s Boston. Unlike many steampunk stories which are set in Victorian England, this one takes place in America and involves such historical icons as Alexander Graham Bell, Thomas Edison, Nikola Tesla, and Harry Houdini. But what really stands out is the character of Granville Woods, an African-American engineer who lived in the same time period. "My stories revolve around the American experience, and you can't do that without having women and people of color in the storyline."

Ms. Holly-Rosing is hoping to raise $25,000 which will cover the cost of the art, coloring, lettering, and production of the last three issues along with shipping, postage, and fees. Like most comic Kickstarters, one of the many incentives is a softbound trade of all six chapters. The Kickstarter campaign will run for thirty days and end on November 15.

To view the webcomic:
http://www.bostonmetaphysicalsociety.com

To view the Kickstarter campaign: http://www.kickstarter.com/projects/488929101/boston-metaphysical-society-webcomic-mini-series

###

If you would like to schedule an interview with Ms. Holly-Rosing or would like more information, please contact her at XXX-XXX-XXXX or email: bostonmetaphysical@gmail.com

The press release for the second Kickstarter took an entirely different tack, but was no less accurate.

SAMPLE PRESS RELEASE #2

Boston Metaphysical Society Webcomic

FOR IMMEDIATE RELEASE

Contact: Madeleine Holly-Rosing
Phone: (XXX) XXX-XXXX
Email: bostonmetaphysical@gmail.com

BOSTON METAPHYSICAL SOCIETY LAUNCHES KICKSTARTER

Steampunk Webcomic Examines American Class Structure

BURBANK, CA. Madeleine Holly-Rosing, writer/creator of the steampunk webcomic, *Boston Metaphysical Society*, announced she would be re-launching her Kickstarter campaign on Wednesday, January 22, to fund the print issue of Chapter 3. "Though we were unsuccessful with our first Kickstarter, we learned a lot about what backers are looking for," Ms. Holly-Rosing commented, "so we scaled back and decided to plan on creating several Kickstarters with smaller goals."

The story is about an ex-Pinkerton detective, his spirit photographer partner, and a genius scientist who battle supernatural forces in late 1800s Boston. Unlike many steampunk stories which are set in Victorian England, this one takes place in America and involves such historical icons as Alexander Graham Bell, Thomas Edison, Nikola Tesla, and Harry Houdini. But what really stands out is its subtle examination of class in America. "I know most people don't like to admit there's a class system in America, but there is. Using the late 1800s as a backdrop allows me as a storyteller to take advantage of the organic conflict between the classes during that time," Ms. Holly-Rosing stated. "I can use the social dynamics of that time period to mirror the social and class issues we deal with today."

Ms. Holly-Rosing is hoping to raise $3,000 to cover printing costs, as well as incentives, shipping, postage, and fees. One of the stretch goals is to print Chapter 4. The Kickstarter campaign will run for thirty days and end on February 21.

To view the webcomic:
http://www.bostonmetaphysicalsociety.com

To view the Kickstarter campaign: http://www.kickstarter.com/

projects/488929101/boston-metaphysical-society-steampunk-comic

###

If you would like to schedule an interview with Ms. Holly-Rosing or would like more information, please contact her by email: bostonmetaphysical@gmail.com

And yes, you do quote yourself. I know it seems a little weird, but that's what you do to make it sound like someone else is interviewing you. So, make sure you sound intelligent.

CHAPTER 9.

PRE-LAUNCH STRATEGY

Pre-launch strategy is as important as your campaign strategy, though even more so. If you are not prepared to launch, don't. Why go through all that stress if you don't have to? Speaking of stress, it's one of the first things you need to prepare for.

YOUR HEALTH

Running a Kickstarter campaign is one of the most stressful things you will ever do. Why? Because you are putting your heart and soul out there for everyone to see and judge. It's also physically hard, because you will find yourself sitting at your desk for hours without a break, so you must take one. You will probably forget to eat. Don't do that. And for those of you who are on any kind of medication, be sure you refill your medication before you launch and make sure you do NOT skip a dose. It will also help to exercise regularly. You won't want to, but do it anyway. It's a great stress reliever and will keep you sane.

TIMING

I've launched campaigns during different times of the year, and I can tell you that it matters. Never, ever launch a campaign over the Thanksgiving and Christmas holidays unless you have a Christmas-type product that you know you can deliver before December25. Also, do not launch in late summer. Everyone is on vacation, and they do not bother to check their email. The best times are mid-January to mid-June, and then after Labor Day until the week before Thanksgiving. (My apologies to overseas readers, but Kickstarter campaigns still run on U.S. holiday schedules.) Also, statistics show that the majority of successful campaigns launch on a Tuesday. I've always launched on a Wednesday because of my own work schedule, but I think launching mid-week is a good idea. The reason being is that on Mondays, people are focused on plowing through that pile of work email that built up over the weekend and don't have time for yours. By the time Friday rolls around, they are mentally out the door; however, you should base this decision on what works for you.

STRETCH GOALS

If you haven't gotten those mapped out yet, now is the time. Have at least two or three and their price point in mind. And remember to BUDGET THEM! In the last year and a half, I have run into a number of campaigns where they have lost money because of their stretch goals. DON'T DO THAT! Be sure you have a large enough stretch goal to pay for whatever that item is along with any additional postage. It also doesn't hurt to add a little buffer so you come out ahead in case of emergencies.

Let me break it down.

For example, say you have made your funding goal of $3,000. You have already decided that your first stretch goal is a cool print or sticker that a friend designed (or you designed) for free. Since you don't have any design costs to worry about, that keeps it pretty simple. (However, if you are photoshopped challenged like I am, then you will probably have to pay someone for designing your stretch goal and build that into your budget.) Next, you have to decide at what price point backers will receive it, and you have to find out how much it will cost to produce the minimum quantity needed to cover those backers. (Remember to only send physical rewards to backers who have pledged to a physical reward.) Let's assume it will cost $150 to produce said stretch goal. Do you then make your stretch goal $3,150? The answer is no. At this particular price break, I'd suggest making the stretch goal at least $3,500. That way you are covered for any printing errors that need to be corrected and any additional postage. If you really want to cover any unexpected expenses, then I'd raise it to $3,750, that way you'll probably end up with a little extra cash that can go to operating expenses or emergencies.

PRESS RELEASES

Now is the time to write and rewrite them. You should also have your list of who you're going to send them to ready to go, as well.

INTERVIEWS AND PODCASTS

Start scheduling interviews and podcasts. Almost all websites are looking for appropriate content, but you do need to contact them at least a month (or more) before you launch. This is not only polite, but often they will have a full schedule and you'll need to be worked in. If it's an email interview (which I prefer), you'll need some time to do a draft, let it sit, then come back to polish it before sending it off. Don't forget to send artwork and anything else they might want to help promote your material.

If you are a non-comics person and you are looking for websites that might be interested in your project, start searching on Google. If you are a film person, use search terms like "film podcasts" or "indie film podcasts." Then, follow up with what you find with a nice email, or better yet, follow them on Twitter and make friends. If you are a genre filmmaker doing sci-fi or fantasy, do the same thing. Repeat for music, biographies, etc. There is a podcast/interview site for everything now. It takes a bit of time, but it will be worth it.

SCHEDULING TWEETS

You know you can send tweets while you sleep, right? This is important to do in order to hit the east coast, Europe, and other time zones for potential backers. If you didn't, then it's time to go and sign up for the free app, Hootsuite (which also has a paid PRO level) or TweetDeck. Both are terrific apps that allow you to schedule tweets when you can't be at your desk. I use the free Hootsuite service, as it's simple and easy to use. What's also nice is that you can link all your social media accounts to Hootsuite to manage all of them in one place if you want to. The only downside is that you can't attach pictures to the scheduled tweets. I like to schedule about one tweet an hour while I'm away from my desk.

CREATE A FACEBOOK EVENT PAGE

By this time you should have created a Facebook page for your project. From here you can create an event page through your Facebook project page. You can do that by either clicking on "Events" in the right-hand column or in the "Upcoming Events" box that shows up about halfway down your page. Be aware that the placement of these fields may change over time, as Facebook has a habit of redesigning pages every year or so.

Upload good cover art for the page and start inviting your Facebook friends. Post images from your project, interviews-whatever is relevant and interesting. You should create the event page about three weeks before you launch.

MAILCHIMP OR SENDINBLUE

Get one of these accounts. Both are fine. I use MailChimp because its basic program is free and easy to use. We will get to the why soon.

GET YOUR VIDEO DONE

By now you should have completed your video and set up your YouTube account with your custom URL. Now it's time to upload it and add the appropriate keywords, like "Kickstarter" or "comics," among others.

CORE EMAIL LIST

Now is the time to build that core email list of backers who you are 99.9% sure will pledge to your project. Remember, they need to make up 25-35% of your funding goal, so this is important. Here's how you do that:

> 1. Write a nice email letter asking people to join your "exclusive" email list for your Kickstarter. Let's call this your "Kickstarter Core Email Letter." Give them a reason to sign up, like "having the first crack at limited early bird specials" in your reward tiers. Or offer them additional incentives like wallpaper or a PDF of a short story (also limited time) – anything to encourage them to sign up that costs you little to no money. You should also tell them this list is just for Kickstarter backers and promise them that they will only receive emails about the Kickstarter and nothing else. By the way, you need to keep that promise. (See Appendix #5 for Sample Email letter.)

> 2. You know that Mail Chimp/Send In Blue account I told you to get? This is why you will need to create what's known as a "List" within Mail Chimp and a form that will allow your future backers to sign up. This will be your Kickstarter Core Email List. Once that is done, there will be a link you can cut and paste into your email letter. That is the link you hope people will click to "Opt-in" to your list.

> I'm sure you're wondering, "Why can't I just type in all those names from the conventions into a MailChimp/SendinBlue list?" Well, you can, but you really want people to "Double Opt-In." There are legal ramifications and the risk of pissing

people off if you add them to a formal list without asking them. And yes, your sign-up sheet at your table is tacit consent, but in this exercise you are trying to put together a list of core backers you can depend on. If someone is willing to take the time to "double opt-in," then you can assume they are serious about following your project.

3. If you haven't already, type up all those emails you gathered from conventions and events to prep them for a mass email. I use a mail merge program in Gmail called "Yet Another Mail Merge" (YAMM). It costs $24 a year to send out 400 emails per day. You first create a draft of your letter and save it. Then, to create a spreadsheet in Google, click on "Drive," select "New" in the upper, left-hand corner, and then chose Google Sheets. Type in your email list and name the document. Click on "Add-ons" on the list across the top of the document, select "Get Add-Ons," and search for "Yet Another Mail Merge." The free version allows you to send up to 50 emails per day. If you need more step-by-step instructions on how to use it, there are numerous video tutorials. I know, because that's how I learned.

Obviously, there are hundreds of mail merge programs out there, but this one has worked well for me. You might find something else out there that you like better or are currently using.

4. Send out your mass Gmail (or other program) email using your "Kickstarter Core Email Letter." You can arrange to have Mail Chimp notify you when people sign up.

5. The next step is to start posting and publicizing your upcoming Kickstarter on Facebook, Twitter, Tumblr, etc., using a modified version of your "Kickstarter Exclusive Email Letter." Be sure to include the MailChimp list link for them to sign up.

6. In MailChimp, create what they refer to as a "Campaign." Essentially, it's an email letter announcing that your Kickstarter has launched. You will need to create that letter using whatever template you prefer prior to launching so it is ready to go after you launch. Don't forget to add the link to your campaign before you send the emails out.

Be aware that there are a few people like me out there who never sign up for these lists, but simply wait until we see that the Kickstarter has launched through social media; however, don't depend on that.

HOW MANY BACKERS DO YOU REALLY NEED?

In the chapter on "Reward Tiers," I talked about your "bread and butter" reward level and how this would most likely be the tier most backers pledged to. The task now is to figure out how many backers you need at that level to make up 25-35% of your funding goal. The reason being is that you need these people to propel you to 35% of your funding goal within three days after launching to maintain momentum and help keep you on the first page of the "Most Popular" category. If you don't, you've made your job a lot harder.

To make this calculation simple, let's use the amount from column F using domestic postage from the chapter on "Postage and Mailing."

As an example, let's assume you have concluded that in order to fund your project, including paying for fees and incentives, you need $3,000. 25% of that is $750. Based on the amount in column F ($18.56), you need 41 backers at that reward tier ($25) to achieve that goal. That is the minimum number of backers you need in your "Kickstarter Core Email List." If you have more, great; if not, go back and work on finding more real potential backers before you launch. Obviously, not everyone will pledge at that level. Some will pledge less and others higher. This is just an average so you get a sense of how many backers you will need and you don't make the mistake of launching too soon.

Even doing this will not guarantee success, but it will increase the probability that you will.

CHAPTER 10.

CAMPAIGN STRATEGY

If you have done everything we've talked about, you are ready to hit the launch button. Take a deep breath and ... click!

Now it's time to set in motion all of the things you've been working on. First thing's first ...

1. Send out an email using your MailChimp "Kickstarter Exclusive Email List" announcing that your Kickstarter has launched. Use the letter that you created in your new "Campaign" and be sure to include a link back to your Kickstarter homepage.

2. Announce your Kickstarter launch on all of your social media accounts. Be sure to tag people who you know are friendly to being tagged and don't mind reposting or retweeting, but do not tag them on every single post.

3. Create a Facebook Event Page if you haven't already. Invite everyone you can think of. Remember to update about any goals reached, updates or other events like signings, Kickstarter parties, post images, etc.

4. Send out a Kickstarter launch email to all of your other email lists. These may (and should) include some on your

Core Email List. It would be a good idea to remove them so they do not receive duplicate emails from you.

5. Email press releases.

6. Cross-Promotion. While you take a break from social media (and you should), search Kickstarter to see if there are any other campaigns going on that might complement yours. Contact them through Kickstarter messaging to see if they would be interested in cross-promoting. What this means is that when you post an update, at the end of the post, you mention these other "fabulous" Kickstarters that your backers might be interested in. (Obviously, you can word it any way you want to.) Never mention more than three at a time, as it dilutes the message and makes your post look like a giant ad. You can also search through Facebook and Twitter for campaigns that might welcome cross-promoting.

During my third campaign, I searched out other steampunk projects and found eight. I contacted all of them. They all agreed except for one. (By the way, don't feel insulted if someone else does not want to cross-promote with you. They could have very valid business reasons that have nothing to do with you or your project.) It worked out very well, as I know I got several more backers from a steampunk game going on at the same time and he got some from me! And I sold some books on the side, as well. It was a win-win!

7. Continue to tweet, post, and repost on the various Facebook groups you have joined, but without overdoing it. After I have sent out my initial launch tweets, I move back to Facebook, then Reddit, then Tumblr, and then back to Twitter again. I try not to send out more than five tweets at a time relating to the Kickstarter, or else it looks spammy. I know it's easy to get carried away, but try to resist the

urge. I do this roughly every few hours. In the meantime, I try to have real conversations with people about topics other than the Kickstarter. Keep those conversations fun, yet interesting.

8. Add a new reward tier (or two) a couple weeks in. This gives you a great update for your Kickstarter and something new to post and tweet about.

9. Post/tweet/update about any milestones reached (i.e., 25% Funded!, 50% Funded!).

10. Post/tweet/update about any interviews, podcasts, and any press at all. This is why it's so important to set up those interviews and podcasts before you launch. Now you have new and fresh stuff to talk about.

11. Check for messages and comments daily and respond to them as quickly as possible.

12. When you get a pledge, thank them both through the Kickstarter messaging system and on Twitter if you know their Twitter handle. They will often retweet it, which is what you want.

13. If you are about two weeks in and you are under 50% funded, consider adding additional incentives to all backers to generate interest and a newsworthy item. It might also be time to add a giveaway during a podcast to garner more listeners who may become backers.

The most important thing to remember is that this is a marathon and not a sprint.

ADDITIONAL PROMOTIONAL OPTIONS

HeadTalker and Thunderclap. These are known as "crowdspeaking" methods of promotion. Essentially, you ask friends, family, and backers to sign up and then on a certain day and time during your campaign, these platforms do one massive Twitter or Facebook blast promoting your campaign. That's done in hopes that your campaign will start trending. The basic package for each is free for the creator though they may charge for extra services. The downside is that whoever signs up to participate has to give them access to your social media account, but ONLY for the date and time in question. I also have not used it, but I have read of those who love it, especially for books, and others who it did nothing for.

Facebook Boosts. These are paid ads. I have not used them, but I know others who were looking for larger funding goals ($20,000 and above) have had success with them.

Project Wonderful Ads. Also another paid advertising option. Once again, I did not use it, but I know others who have with varied results.

Twitter Ads. You always have that option, but I think it's unnecessary.

SPAM WARNING

As soon as you launch, you will start receiving messages through the Kickstarter and Indiegogo messaging system and to your email from marketing firms promising that they can get you exposure, backers, etc. Ignore them. Most of them are scams and if you're looking to raise under $10,000, you don't need them if you've done your homework.

CHAPTER 11.

THE PSYCHOLOGY OF A CAMPAIGN

I'm not a professional psychologist, but I do know a thing or two about how people perceive whether or not your Kickstarter is going to be successful even if you think you are doing okay.

While you're tweeting, posting, or doing podcasts, you also need to be keeping track of your progress. You can do that using Kicktraq.com, but be aware that the first few days are always skewed in an upward trend and you need to wait a week for the real trend to reveal itself. I like Kicktraq because it has mini-charts that tell you how much pledge money you need to make every day to achieve your goal.

Kickstarter utilizes the power of game theory with its all-or-nothing environment. Like eBay, once a person pledges, they are now emotionally invested in your project and will often try to get others to push you over your goal; however, you have to be near enough to your goal as the clock runs down for that to happen.

Be aware that people can pull out their pledge at any time. (There are a few exceptions which are noted later.) A good example is what happened in my third Kickstarter. It was Monday of our last week in the campaign. We were over 90% funded at $7,065. Good, right? Well, on my way to work, I noticed that we had dropped below $7,000 between the time I left home and the time I arrived at work. Three people had backed out. It happens, and there's nothing you can do about it but move on; however, being that it was the last week, I was very concerned that there would be the perception that something had gone wrong with the campaign and people would jump ship. Being over $7,000 at this late date was critical in the perception that this was going to be a successful campaign. It could have also affected our ranking within the Kickstarter algorithm, which I'll explain in a moment.

So, what did I do? I got on the phone to my husband and told him to pledge $100, just enough to get us back over the $7,000 mark. And yes, relatives can pledge, but you cannot. After that, we had no problem making our goal, but it's always a little unsettling to have three people back out in one day.

KICKSTARTER ALGORITHM

I have no doubt that you've noticed that you can search for projects under different categories and types. I am sure, though I have no empirical proof, that the most looked at sub-category is "Most Popular." And the two most viewed pages under "Most Popular" are the first and the last page. Want to know why? People like to see what's doing well and who the train wrecks are. If at all possible, you want your project to be on the first page of the "Most Popular," as most people do not look beyond the first page. (Think about it. When you do a Google search, how many times do you go to the next page, let alone the third?)

The way you do that is to have a constant stream of pledges throughout your campaign. It doesn't have to be a huge amount per day, but just enough to keep you visible on that first page.

The reason I mention all of this is that it appears that Kickstarter may have an internal algorithm that boosts you up in the rankings if it appears you are trending toward make your funding goal. Remember, they are in the business of making money. If you succeed, they get their 5%.

THERE BE EVILDOERS OUT THERE

There is a term coined by Thomas Pratt, the co-creator of *Shadowbinders* (A Steampunk Webcomic), called a "Kicktroller." He and his wife Kambrea (co-creator) had the unfortunate experience to run into one.

Their campaign goal was $25,000 and they were doing okay, but not great. Though they were running it over the Thanksgiving holidays, they received a pledge of $10,000. Pretty exciting. According to Kambrea, Thomas contacted the backer directly, as well as Kickstarter, to make sure it was real. The guy claimed it was and he loved the project. Then, over Thanksgiving, he started to reduce his pledge in small increments, until finally over the long weekend the $10,000 was gone. Now, Thomas is stuck with a downward trending campaign (in a big way) and no way to recover. Their campaign failed, but they re-strategized and re-launched the following year to resounding success.

Other articles I've read discussed how other Kicktrollers would pledge a large amount and then pull it all right before time ran out, causing the campaign to fail. Others have kept it in until after the project was funded, but then disputed the charges and then you're still stuck paying the fees.

I wrote a letter to Kickstarter in 2013 asking them to establish a policy on how to deal with Kicktrollers. My husband and I suggested a couple of things:

> 1. The creator has the right to refuse any pledge and can have it removed from the total amount before the funding period is over.

> 2. Anyone who pledges an amount greater than $5,000 must allow 5-10% of that money to be held in escrow. If the campaign fails, the money is released. If it's successful, they are charged even if they do pull out at the last minute.

I did receive a letter back from Kickstarter thanking me and letting me know that the letter would be put to good use. (I have a feeling this was a hot topic for them internally at the time.) I'm hoping that the letter (amongst others I'm sure) did have some small effect, as their policy under *Terms of Use* has since changed (effective October 19, 2014) to read:

> • *In some cases we'll reserve the charge on your card. Kickstarter and its payment partners may authorize or reserve a charge on your credit card (or whatever payment method you use) for any amount up to the full pledge, at any time between the pledge and the collection of funds.*

> • *You can change or cancel your pledge at any time before the project's funding deadline (with one exception). You can increase, decrease, or cancel your pledge at any time during the campaign, with one exception. During the last 24 hours of the campaign, you can't decrease or cancel your pledge without contacting customer support first — if that action would drop the project below its funding goal. Once the project has been funded, you can only cancel or change your pledge by making special arrangements directly with the creator.*

Unfortunately, trolls still lurk out there, as in 2015 the game, *Dimension Drive*, was €7000 below their funding goal, and near the end of their campaign a pledge came in for that exact amount. The creators were still celebrating when Kickstarter recognized it as fraudulent and the system pulled the money from the campaign. Needless to say, it was too late for the creators to have time to find the money elsewhere, and the campaign failed. Obviously, if they were €7000 away from their goal toward the end of their campaign, there was little chance of it succeeding, but the troll gave false hope and added to an already emotionally exhausting experience.

More recently, I've talked to other creators where Kickstarter had caught a bogus pledge and removed it, so I know they are trying to stay on top of it; however, I have a feeling it's like playing a game of whack-a-mole.

CHAPTER 12.

SOCIAL MEDIA ETIQUETTE (OR HOW NOT TO ANNOY PEOPLE)

It's hard not to overstep boundaries when you've worked so hard on a project and you want your Kickstarter to succeed; however, sometimes, you can be too aggressive and that can put people off.

Here are some suggestions:

1. Do not tag everyone you know on every single post or tweet. I know a very talented gentleman who tagged over 25 people on every single Kickstarter Facebook post, including me. It was so annoying that I stopped wanting to help him.

2. If someone new follows you during the campaign, thank them for following, and then engage in a polite conversation that is not related to the Kickstarter. I think it is better to wait until you've actually had some interaction with them before you ask. Get to know them at least a little bit. Obviously, some people won't care and will either ignore you or retweet you while others may block you. Also, if someone accepts your friend request on Facebook, don't immediately send them a message asking them to donate to your campaign. It's just rude.

I did get a bit spammy in my first Kickstarter, and I was politely called on it on Twitter. I promptly stopped and had a nice conversation with the person who pointed it out to me. I doubt she backed the project, but for anyone who was watching our feed then, they would have seen how I handled her suggestions. Nothing in social media is private, so act like everyone is reading your stuff: good and bad.

3. If someone backs out, don't hunt them down on social media to find out why. Respect their decision and move on.

4. If you post about your Kickstarter in your Facebook groups, and you will, occasionally, someone will accuse you of spamming even if you have followed the rules of the group. If it's the moderator, just do what they ask and don't argue. If it's other people being trolls, ignore them and don't respond. If it gets weird or ugly, just delete the entire post and move on. Do not engage them, as it adds fuel to the fire and you don't want any negativity surrounding your Kickstarter. It's bad publicity.

And if you're wondering, it did happen to me. Another person in the group defended me and I received no complaints from the moderator, but I decided it was just getting stupid and I deleted the entire post.

CHAPTER 13.

FULFILLMENT

Congratulations! You made your goal. Now what?

First, you thank all of your backers profusely and tell them that you are taking a short break from social media to get some much-needed rest. But you'll be back soon with updates on the progress of the project.

Next, you wait for Stripe to clear your funds. It takes about two weeks, and be aware that not all of your pledges will clear. Some people will have expired credit cards they've forgotten to update, which will eventually clear as Stripe will notify them and they will have the opportunity to update their information. Others ... well, they won't care, and you'll never see that money.

Let's imagine it is a perfect world and your project is completed by the time you said it would be. Then, there's the reality. Very few projects are completed on time. We try, but something always happens. Most backers will understand as long as you keep them informed. Don't leave your progress a mystery; it's just rude. These people gave you money. The least you could do is let them know what you're doing with it. As you work on your project, be sure to send updates no more than every two weeks, and make sure you have something to say. (Every week can be too much and people will stop reading them.) There are exceptions, especially if there is something important to announce.

That being said, once your comics, games, books, or whatever are about to arrive at your front door to be shipped out, you need to be prepared.

Here is a list to help you make sure you're ready to handle the next step in your Kickstarter project:

1. Send out the backer surveys that are available through your Kickstarter Backer Report Page to obtain their address, email, phone number, preferred name to use on your "Thank You" page or website, or whatever other information you need. (Remember, you need the phone number of your international backers in order to process their postage.)

2. Once the surveys have come back to you, download the backer information onto a spreadsheet. I only use the spreadsheets to help me pack up rewards for the different tiers, then I check them off as I finish. It's easier for me to copy their name and address from Kickstarter and paste it onto my label template in Word, and then print that out. This is an example of what the survey response looks like:

Survey response
Responded on Dec. 11 2014
Address updated on Apr. 11 2015
Name & address
Caitlin O'Sullivan
247 Dorchester St.
Boston, MA 02196
USA

What name would you like on the Kickstarter Thank You Wall?
Caitlin O'Sullivan

Others may have better ways of doing it based on how well you know Excel. If you do, great.

3. Order packaging/shipping material.

4. Have storage space ready.

5. Have a place to assemble your packages. Get help if you need it.

6. Ship in stages. Don't try to do it all at once, as it can be overwhelming, especially if you're doing it by yourself.

7. Some post offices require appointments if you are bringing in more than 30 or more packages at a time. Call your local post office to find out.

8. Check Kickstarter for messages and comments daily until you have shipped out all of your rewards.

9. Though I mentioned it before, it's worth mentioning Stamps.com and Endicia.com again as a way to pre-pay your postage, then just drop it off at the post office.

10. Never underestimate the time and labor in fulfilling rewards. In my last Kickstarter, I had about 200 packages to mail. Every afternoon for a good week, I labeled, signed, and packed about 30-50 a day on my living room floor. Then I headed out to the post office to mail them. Once you get there, it can take up to 30 minutes for a clerk to process up to 50 packages. So, plan for that.

PROFESSIONAL FULFILLMENT COMPANIES

If your campaign has succeeded beyond your wildest dreams, then you might want to consider hiring a professional fulfillment company to help with all of the above. I have never used one myself, but if I had over 500 backers, then I would strongly consider it.

Since crowdfunding has become big business, a number of fulfillment companies have popped up. Here are a few you might want to check out, though I have no doubt there are more of them:

- BackerKit/Shipwire
- Amazon
- ShipMonk
- Fulfillrite
- Floship

I can't stress enough that you should research any fulfillment company thoroughly before you hire them.

CHAPTER 14.

DEALING WITH SUCCESS

How hard can dealing with success be, you ask?

Well, there is the etiquette side of this. Be humble, be appreciative, and be thankful. Help promote other campaigns that aren't doing as well as yours. That doesn't mean you have to pledge, but a post here, a tweet there, and even a little cross-promotion can go a long way in making you look like a decent human being. (Cross-promote only if it's appropriate. If you have a PG-rated project and theirs is NSFW, then you might not want to do it.) Plus, by being generous, supportive, and helpful to other campaigns, they may return the favor when you need it later. And you probably will if you launch another campaign.

The independent creator community, whether it be comics, film, music, or anything else, is made up of small communities, and people remember how they are treated. Be one of the good guys and gals.

Then, there's the money issue. I've consulted with a number of campaigns who exceeded their wildest dreams. For a few, they had never had that much money at their disposal before, and it was very tempting to start paying off student loans, credit card debt, etc. A few did and when it came time to ship out rewards, they had run out of cash to pay for postage. And there are the taxes you'll have to pay. That's a problem you don't want to have. Here are my thoughts on the matter:

1. Take a deep breath and wait before you do anything.
2. Crunch your numbers for fulfillment again. Even if it looks like you could pay off the loans or debt and still handle sending out all the rewards, don't do it quite yet. And here's why — Something always happens and it's usually postage going up which you didn't figure into your budget. You need to have some buffer to take care of contingencies because they always happen.
3. Set aside money for taxes.
4. Perhaps pay off a portion of your loan or debt, but do not spend it all. I'm sorry to sound like your parents, but you need to be responsible. Remember, you are playing with other people's money.
5. And last of all … Be proud of yourself and what you have accomplished. It is a big deal.

CHAPTER 15.

TAXES

I've gotten a lot of questions about taxes, so let me say this up front — I am not a tax expert and I cannot give tax advice. I would suggest working with a tax professional who has experience with artists, writers, and creator types, as our income has some gray areas. That being said, usually, any money derived from a crowdfunding campaign is considered income and is, therefore, taxable; however, and this is where your tax expert comes in, you might have enough deductibles to help offset your tax bill. Some of your funds may also be considered a "gift" and are, therefore, tax free, but once again, consult your tax professional.

Here are some general tips:

• Try to use the money from your campaign to produce your project in the same year that you received it.

• Be sure to keep good records and receipts.

• Determine the retail value of your reward in case you end up paying sales tax.

A note on sales tax: Most states haven't figured out how to deal with crowdfunding and sales taxes yet which is another reason to consult with a tax attorney or a tax professional who has.

If you live outside of the United States, different rules may apply, so be sure to check with your local tax authorities.

This information is intended to set you on the right path, but it is up to you to obtain complete information from a tax professional.

CHAPTER 16.

WHAT IF YOU FAIL? TURNING FAILURE INTO ADVANTAGE

Failing to reach your goal after putting your heart and soul into it can be devastating. The reasons you failed could be that you thought you were prepared, but you really weren't. Or it could simply be due to life emergencies. In fact, if you have a family emergency, it might just be better to inform what backers you have as to what's going on and cancel the campaign. Your health and your family's health come first. Whatever you do, don't beat yourself up over it. Use this time to take a step back and review your project to see how it can be reshaped and re-strategized for a future campaign.

For most failed campaigns, you're going to know if you're not going to make it just by watching the trends. There is always a chance to reverse it, as I talked about in the "Campaign Strategy" section, but if you are only 30-35% funded three weeks in, you are probably not going to make it. Next comes the decision to cancel or let it ride to the end. I have a definite opinion on that.

I'm a strong believer in controlling the message you send to the outside world. It's basic marketing. If you just let your Kickstarter end without contacting your backers and disappear into the void, it looks bad. Even if you fail, you must be humble toward the backers who supported you, yet appear organized, competent, and have a spine of steel. That's why I think you should let your Kickstarter continue until the last 24 hours of the campaign or when you start seeing backers withdraw their pledges, whichever comes first. Here's why:

First, you want to build a database of known, willing backers. Letting the campaign continue as long as possible will benefit you in the long run; however, if you see backers withdrawing their pledges, you should cancel before you lose any more. You don't want to let too many potential future backers flee, as you can still contact them through Kickstarter when you re-launch. This is called data mining, and you need this data (i.e., names and ability to contact). Once they have backed out, you cannot contact them. Only if you are fully funded does Kickstarter allow you to download their contact information.

However, when you do cancel, don't click on that button and walk away without any kind of thanks to the people who did back you.

Second, have a plan and let your backers know what it is. It could be to re-launch for a smaller funding goal and scaled-down project. Or it could be that you decided not to use Kickstarter at all. Maybe you've decided to self-fund or use Indiegogo. Whatever you decide, don't cut off the people who believed in you.

Below is the letter I wrote to backers after I canceled my first Kickstarter.

Dear Supporters:

There's less than 15 hours left and we're at 30%. So, I'm calling it. Not that I want to, but this Kickstarter is over. But don't worry, friends. Boston Metaphysical Society *isn't down or out. We are simply going to regroup after getting some rest and preparing for the holidays.*

I will say, though, that each and every one of you is 1000% awesome for getting behind it, and believing in it, and sharing it, reposting, tweeting, and blogging. And I want to thank every one of you from the bottom of my heart for backing this project. I was awed by the number of people I have never met who contributed to the Kickstarter. Your belief in this project helps keep me going and for that I am truly grateful.

My husband and I have already started to assemble the parts for the re-launch, which is going to take place in mid-January. And then just like now, I'll need your help. Our tentative plan is to launch a Kickstarter to print issue three with a stretch goal to print issue four. And I'm pretty sure that the tea reward is going to be in the mix.

However, the first thing I need to ask you to do is to sign up for the new mailing list. This will become the main way I'll communicate after the fact about things that are very timing-specific. I repeat: Please sign up for the mailing list. The Facebook page is still the place to go to see fun things and updates to art and such, but posts there don't get seen by everyone in the group unless you are very active (or pay to have them shown). So, be sure to get on the mailing list, and I promise to only talk about Boston Metaphysical Society *and related projects on there.*

As a reminder, since the Kickstarter project did not make it past the 100% mark for its goal, no money is being withdrawn from your accounts. Your money stays safely where it is. Canceling just means we won't be collecting on the pledges we currently have, nor can new pledges be received. If we were to reboot, we would have to ask you for your pledge again at that time. The Boston Metaphysical Society *Kickstarter page will still exist, but only as an archive of the project itself. Finally, have a wonderful holiday season, and we'll be back next year.*

All the best,

Madeleine Holly-Rosing
Writer/Creator, Boston Metaphysical Society

Note that I first thanked all of my backers, then talked about our future plans, and then asked them to sign up for our new mailing list—three times! This was very important as it became my Kickstarter Core Email List that I used when we re-launched two months later.

As a side note, if you do decide to re-launch, do it at least a month after you cancel, but no more than three months. Even if you know exactly what your strategy is going to be, you have to allow time for people to at least think that you have weighed your options and made a thoughtful and considered decision.

I remember a Kickstarter to fund a webcomic by a young man which I backed. It wasn't a well-thought-out campaign, yet he wasn't asking for a lot of money and I admired his tenaciousness. He was asking for a little over $1,000. He didn't reach his goal, and re-launched less than a week later for less money. This left me with the impression that he did not take the time to re-examine and re-think his campaign, so I did not back it again.

On the other hand, if you wait too long, people will forget you existed. That's why I recommend re-launching within three months.

CHAPTER 17.

FINAL THOUGHTS

This is a lot of information to take in, so I recommend re-reading the book and taking notes that are applicable to your project. I've tried to strip crowdfunding down to its essentials to make it easier to access. Be sure to use the worksheets in the back as a guide to help you. Give yourself plenty of time to plan and don't rush anything. It's better to take your time and build your list of potential backers than try to find them after you have launched.

Good luck!

ABOUT THE AUTHOR

Madeleine Holly-Rosing is a graduate of the UCLA MFA Program in Screenwriting, where she won the Sloan Fellowship for screenwriting as well as other awards. She has also won the Gold Aurora and Bronze Telly for a PSA she wrote and was produced by Women In Film.

Her comic, *Boston Metaphysical Society,* was nominated for Best Comic/Graphic at the 2014 Geekie Awards and was nominated for a 2012 Airship Award, as well as a 2013, 2014, and a 2015 Steampunk Chronicle Reader's Choice Award. Her novella, *Steampunk Rat,* was also nominated for a 2013 Steampunk Chronicle Reader's Choice Award.

Madeleine has run four successful crowdfunding campaigns for her comic and not only has been teaching a course at Pulp Fiction Books and Comics in Culver City, CA, since 2015, but has guest lectured at Scriptwriters Network, DreamWorks Animation, and other institutions.

Formerly a nationally ranked epeé fencer, she has competed nationally and internationally and is an avid reader of steampunk, science fiction, fantasy, and historical military fiction.

Madeleine lives with her rocket scientist husband David and two rescue dogs: Ripley and Bishop.

Please follow her on:
Website: http://www.bostonmetaphysicalsociety.com
Facebook: https://www.facebook.com/
BostonMetaphysicalSocietyComic
Twitter: http://www.twitter.com/mhollyrosing
LinkedIn: https://www.linkedin.com/in/madeleinehollyrosing

APPENDIX #1: SAMPLE LIST OF WEBSITES FROM WHICH TO REQUEST A REVIEW (COMICS)

Fanbase Press

FanboyNation

Comics Bulletin

Rhymes With Geek

Associated Geekery

Geeks with Capes and Wives

The Legal Geeks

A Place to Hang Your Cape

Word of the Nerd

Comic Wow!

ReadComicBooks.net

Comics and Cashmere

The Geek Girl Project

The Good Man Project

Curiosity of a Social Misfit

Comic Book and Movie Reviews

Women Write About Comics

Fanboys Anonymous

Bag and Bored

(Note: This list is subject to change due to life and other circumstances.)

APPENDIX #2: SAMPLE LIST OF WEBSITES FOR INTERVIEWS/PODCASTS

Comics Bulletin

~~Fanbase Press~~

ODNT YouTube Channel

Just Joshing

~~Rhymes With Geek~~

Womb Mates

Robots Attack

~~Associated Geekery~~

~~Geeks with Capes and Wives~~

~~The Legal Geeks~~

Next Level Geek

Atomic Moo

~~Word of the Nerd~~

Amanda Gilliam Presents

(Note: This list is subject to change due to life and other circumstances.)

APPENDIX #3: KICKSTARTER SPOTLIGHT LIST (COMICS)

(Email a request first as guidelines change.)

Fanbase Press

Comics Bulletin

Geeks of Doom

ComicAttack

Comics Beat

Pipedream Comics

Outright Geekery

PopCultHQ

Comicbooked

Graphic Policy

Multiversity Comics

Stash My Comics

Bag and Bored

Rogues Portal

Pop Culture Pipebomb

Comics Heating Up

The Legal Geeks

Geek News Network

Geeky Cool

Comics Bulletin

Comic Book Resources

Comic Wow!

Bleeding Cool

Geek News Network

LA Weekly

Your local newspaper

Your alumni newsletter

Comic Creator News

Comics Beat

(Note: This list is subject to change due to life and other circumstances.)

APPENDIX #4: SAMPLE CONTACT EMAILS FOR PRESS RELEASES

---

1. Dear _____: (Warm)*
I did an interview with you last year about my comic, *Boston Metaphysical Society*, and I was wondering if I could submit a press release about diversity in comics and my newly launched Kickstarter to be published on your website.
Thanks so much.
Best,
Madeleine

2. Dear _____: (Cold)**

I'm writing to see if you'd be interested in doing a story on my steampunk supernatural webcomic, *Boston Metaphysical Society*, and our Kickstarter campaign.
The webcomic is about an ex-Pinkerton detective and his spirit photographer partner who battle supernatural forces in late 1800s Boston. Think "Steampunk *X-Files*."
I've attached a press release for your convenience.

Thanks for your time.

Best,

Madeleine Holly-Rosing
Writer/Creator
Boston Metaphysical Society Webcomic

*Warm means you have had some contact with that person in the past, so the letter can be more informal.
**Cold means you have never had contact with this person before.

APPENDIX #5: OTHER SAMPLE MARKETING EMAILS

Hi, _____:

Thank you for stopping by the *Boston Metaphysical Society* table at the Alternative Press Expo (APE). It was great to meet you.

I have some pretty exciting news ... the comic has been nominated for Best Comic/Graphic Novel at the Geekie Awards this year!

Even more importantly, I will be launching a Kickstarter campaign on August 13 to fund the production and printing of Chapter 5. If you are interested in receiving exclusive Kickstarter updates, please sign up here: *Boston Metaphysical Society* Kickstarter Updates.

Also, Chapters 3 and 4 of the comic are now available for sale. You can purchase it at the *Boston Metaphysical* Store along with the other chapters, posters, and fun steampunk swag.

If you're in the mood to dive more deeply into the Boston Metaphysical universe, there are also short stories and novellas available on Kindle, Nook, Smashwords (all ereaders), and DrivethruFiction (PDF).

Thank you so much for your time.

Best,
Madeleine Holly-Rosing
Writer/Creator
Boston Metaphysical Society Comic

APPENDIX #6: ADDITIONAL REFERENCE MATERIAL (COMICS AND OTHER TYPES OF PROJECTS)

FOR PROMOTION:

Other websites that might be useful for promotion are:

- Kicktraq
- CrowdfundingPR
- The Best Crowdfunding Community (Google+)
- Kickstarter Subreddit on Reddit
- And, of course, your own blog.

FOR EDUCATIONAL RESOURCES:

On Facebook, I have found the following groups to be useful:

- Kickstarter Best Practices – It's game centric, but educational.
- The Best of Kickstarter
- Kickstarter Comic Books
- Kickstarter and Indiegogo Worldwide Community
- Back This Kickstarter
- Patreon Tips (Some of the threads can be interesting.)

OTHER:

- Kickstarterforum.org (It also has an Indiegogo subgroup.)
- ComixLaunch
- Crowd101.com
- LinkedIn (Numerous groups)

(Note: This list is subject to change due to life and other circumstances.)

WORKSHEET #1 – Project Costs

A	B	C	D	E	F	G	H
Reward Tier	Tier Price	Cost to Produce The Reward	Packaging	Postage	Kickstarter/ Stripe Fees – 10%	Total Costs (Add C thru F)	Money available for product creation (Subtract G from B)
#1 – Domestic							
#1 - International							
#2 – Domestic							
#2 - International							
#3 - Domestic							
#3 - International							
#4 - Domestic							
#4 - International							
#5 - Domestic							
#5 - International							
#6 - Domestic							
#6 - International							
#7 - Domestic							
#7 - International							
#8 - Domestic							
#8 - International							
#9 - Domestic							
#9 - International							

Legend: Gray shaded area is for costs.

Note: You will probably have more than nine (9) reward tiers.

WORKSHEET #2 – REWARD TIERS

Use this page to jot down ideas for reward tier names and what you can offer potential backers.

Tier Names	Reward

WORKSHEET #3 – STRETCH GOALS

Use this sheet to jot down ideas for Stretch Goals and how much they cost along with any added shipping costs.

Stretch Goals	Additional Costs

Made in the USA
San Bernardino, CA
26 September 2017